Every

Everyman
and be thy guide

Women in Love:

Heroines in Verse

Selected and edited by

DAVID and SANDRA HOPKINS

University of Bristol

EVERYMAN
J. M. Dent · London

This edition first published by Everyman Paperbacks in 2000
Selection, introduction and other critical apparatus
© J. M. Dent 2000

J. M. Dent
Orion Publishing Group
Orion House
5 Upper St Martin's Lane
London WC2H 9EA

Typeset by Deltatype Ltd, Birkenhead, Merseyside
Printed in Great Britain by
The Guernsey Press Co. Ltd, Guernsey, C. I.

British Library Cataloguing-in-Publication
Data is available on request

ISBN 0 460 88213 9

Contents

Note on the Anthology and its Editors

This unique anthology presents depictions of female figures in a wide range of English verse – narrative, dramatic and lyric, original and translated – from the Middle Ages to the late nineteenth century. The emphasis is on the variety of women's reactions to the passion of love – whether joyful, idealizing, horrified, deceitful, resigned, noble, curious, or reflective. The collection juxtaposes familiar material with less well-known items, and encompasses a wide variety of tones and moods, from heroic pathos to bawdy comedy. The passages all present moments in which a woman's thoughts are rendered, or her presence imagined, with particular dramatic vividness. The women depicted range from nobly born heroines of myth and legend to more ordinary and everyday figures. The result is a comprehensive presentation – moving, sobering and amusing by turns – of the joys, fears, hopes and disappointments of women in love.

DAVID HOPKINS is Reader in English Poetry at the University of Bristol. His publications include editions of Cowley (with Tom Mason) and Dryden (with Paul Hammond), an anthology of poets' writings about their peers, a book (with Tom Mason) about the arts of poetry and poetry-reading, an edited collection of essays (with Charles Martindale) on the influence of Horace in English literature, and selections from Dryden, Homer and Ovid in the Everyman's Poetry Series.

SANDRA HOPKINS read English at King's College, London, and has taught a wide range of English and American literature at school and adult-education level. She is a recognized teacher in Continuing Education (English) at the University of Bristol, and contributed a chapter on Dickens to *Problems for Feminist Criticism*, edited by Sally Minogue (Routledge, 1990).

Introduction

This anthology presents depictions of female figures in a wide range of English verse – lyric, narrative and dramatic, original and translated – from the fourteenth to the late nineteenth century. The cut-off point was partly prompted by considerations of copyright, but also by the fact that the subject-matter of the anthology has, over the last century, tended to become the preserve of novelists rather than poets. The collection focuses on women experiencing the passion of love in a variety of ways: joyful, horrified, idealizing, deceitful, resigned, noble, curious, reflective. The 'love' in question is, frequently, a violent and consuming passion, closer to the Greek *eros* or the Roman *amor* than to the more tender and selfless emotions that the term sometimes suggests. The portrayals encompass a wide variety of tones and moods, from heroic pathos to bawdy comedy. The emphasis is on poems and passages that present a female figure dramatically, whether in the first person, or by particularly vivid description or evocation. Love lyrics as such, and poems in the poet's first person, have generally been excluded, though the anthology does include a few items in which the personal experience of the poet is presented in thinly disguised form. Many of the items are extracts from longer works, but have – or so we hope – sufficient local life and power to survive temporary excerption from their original context (brief headnotes give concise indications of the passages' original setting). The volume is organized alphabetically by heroine. Anyone who reads the anthology through from beginning to end will thus experience a kaleidoscope of tone, style and historical provenance, and a wide variety of female types, from the grandes dames of myth, legend and history, to more ordinary, everyday figures. The result is a comprehensive portrayal – moving, amusing, awe-inspiring and sobering by turns – of the fears, hopes and disappointments of women in love.

Portrayals of women in poetry – particularly by male poets – have often been accused of presenting reductive stereotypes which tell us more about the fantasies, needs, fears and will-to-power of men

than about the true characteristics of female nature. According to
such a view, women are commonly represented as a series of 'types'
– the Passive Victim, the Seductive Temptress, the Shrewish
Harridan, the Ugly Crone, the Lustful Lecher, the Saintly Virgin, the
Selfless Mother, the Spoilt Child, the Jealous Jilt, the Warlike
Amazon, the Bookish Blue-Stocking – each one of which ultimately
reveals more about the hopes and dreads of their male (or male-
influenced) creators than about the female race that they seek to
epitomize. Male depictions of women, it is sometimes claimed, are a
form of 'ventriloquism' or 'appropriation', a kind of domination, in
which women's predicament is rendered exclusively in terms of
their relations with men, and which thereby reinforces the
suffering and sense of entrapment which women have, historically,
been forced to endure at male hands.

Anyone browsing in this anthology will notice immediately that
the extracts – many of them by male poets – do, indeed, present
women experiencing a series of recurrent predicaments, and
voicing a series of recurrent anxieties, aspirations, joys and desires.
Women are, in these extracts, repeatedly seen lamenting their ill-
treatment at the hands of former lovers, entertaining idealized
visions of their perfect partner, and compromising, in various ways,
with the social and ethical constraints of the communities in which
they live. But presentations of recurrent human experiences are not
necessarily merely appropriative or stereotypical in tendency.
When reflecting on the distinctive qualities that constitute Shake-
speare's supreme excellence as a writer, Samuel Johnson noted
how Shakespeare finely 'discriminates' his characters and keeps
them uniquely 'distinct from each other'. Yet, at the same time,
Johnson maintained, Shakespeare's characters are not merely
idiosyncratic. 'In the writings of other poets,' he wrote, 'a character
is too often an individual; in those of Shakespeare it is commonly a
species.' Shakespeare's characters, for Johnson, are 'the genuine
progeny of common humanity, such as the world will always
supply and observation will always find'. Their 'common' qualities
do not mean that they are mere stereotypes. Their creator has
endowed them with a freedom and independence of imagined life
which makes them seem embodiments or concentrations of
archetypal human experience, rather than merely reductive
impositions of authorial viewpoint or will. The passages in this
anthology, at their best, aspire to a similar combination of

individual distinctiveness and generality of implication and appli-
cation – qualities which depend more on the imaginative capacities
and writerly skill of their authors than on whether those authors
happened to be male or female.

The passages avoid stereotypicality partly by virtue of the
complexity and subtlety of the responses that they elicit from the
reader. Hardly ever are we allowed to rest secure in any simple or
single reponse to the woman portrayed. Even those passages that
come close to satire – such as Gay's portrayal of the jealous
coquette, Lydia, or Byron's of Donna Julia, or Crabbe's of Arabella –
are not merely superior or censorious in tone. Nor is the ardent or
idealized love of women presented as straightforwardly admirable,
or condemned as escapist fantasy or naïve wish-fulfilment. Tenny-
son's Elaine is, in some senses, submissive, and dies for love, but she
also boldly defies custom and decorum in the absoluteness of her
declared passion for Lancelot. And Keats, in rendering the emotions
and behaviour of Madeline on St Agnes' Eve, is alert both to the
dangers and pains and the attractions of dream-like love-fantasy.
In Amy Levy's depiction, Xantippe (the proverbial 'type' of the
shrewish wife) honestly admits the conflict between her recogni-
tion of Socrates' great mental powers, and the fact that she finds
him physically undesirable. Chaucer's Wife of Bath might seem
simply to embody male fears of a shrew endowed with formidable
sexual appetites, but she displays a subversively challenging
energy, and constantly surprising range of emotional susceptibil-
ities which belie this stereotype. Chaucer's Criseyde – notorious for
her infidelity – displays a genuine uncertainty about her own
motives and feelings, and a painful realization of the cost of her
behaviour, together with self-delusion and specious self-justifica-
tion. Milton's Dalilah justifies her notorious betrayal of Samson
with an eloquence and cogency which demonstrate the inextrica-
ble intertwining of passion, deception and self-delusion. Pope's
Penelope is the archetype of the loyal, enduring wife, but also
displays hard-headed resourcefulness and cunning in her demand
for proof positive that the stranger claiming to be her long-lost
husband is indeed Ulysses. Chaucer's Griselda accepts her hus-
band's behaviour without recrimination, but does so with a clear-
sighted and unsentimental recognition of Walter's appalling
harshness to her. Cartwright's Ariadne and Dryden's Dido are
depicted as lamenting victims, but they express their feelings not in
a tone of helpless acceptance, but with formidable violence and

vindictiveness towards the heroes who have deserted them. Shakespeare's Juliet and Elizabeth Browning's 'Portuguese Lady' seem to epitomize single-minded devotion to their lovers, but Juliet has misgivings about her premature revelation of her feelings to Romeo, and the Portuguese Lady expresses scepticism about the possibility of articulating her passion in the very act of making the attempt. Shakespeare's Cleopatra gives rapturous expression to her feelings for an Antony who, many readers have felt, squares uncomfortably with the figure we see for ourselves, and is, perhaps, only a figment of her imagination – albeit a glorious one. Shakespeare's Viola and Spenser's Britomart both appear at first sight confidently resourceful heroines, yet we witness the great pain and insecurity that both suffer in their love. Elizabeth Browning's Aurora Leigh seems the self-reliant, feminist rationalist, yet comes to believe that her own assertions of independence are tainted with self-regard, and a lack of truth to her own most acutely felt emotions.

The love depicted in this anthology is, frequently, an unruly and intractable emotion, more productive of pain, frustration, fear and turmoil than of happiness or equanimity. It confounds other human bonds and moral imperatives: friendship, family, loyalty, self-esteem, common sense, and the demands of society and religion. Nahum Tate's Medea, for example, is torn between her desire for Jason and her sense of loyalty to her father's kingdom. Webster's Duchess of Malfi, in love with her steward, is conscious that the promptings of her heart conflict with her aristocratic status. Dryden's Sigismonda defiantly defends her sexual needs, and her love for Guiscardo, against her father's powerfully stated opposition. The same poet's Myrrha is thrown by her incestuous desire for her father into direct conflict with all 'normal' moral and human impulses. Fairfax's Erminia is forced to compromise her own Moslem religion because of her love for the crusader knight, Tancred. Byron's Francesca da Rimini falls in love with her own brother-in-law, and is punished in Hell for her transgression. The passion of Marlowe's Hero for the young Leander forces her to forget her vow of chastity as 'Venus' Nun'. Shakespeare's Helena feels demeaned by her 'unwomanly' desire to court the reluctant Demetrius. Clare's milkmaid, Dolly, is seduced by gifts from a country fair, and loses her virginity. Browning's Ottima is prompted to murder by the power of her passion, and loves Sebald all the more for his complicity in her crime. Pope's Andromache is led by forebodings about her own future to compromise her husband Hector's obligations as protector and champion of his native Troy. Eloisa's love for Abelard causes her to subsume into her passion the religious feelings to which she should be primarily devoted. Guinevere's adultery with Lancelot destroys the civilization of the Round Table. And, like Helen of Troy, Guinevere is fully aware of the wider cost of her personal infidelity.

Women in love are shown in this anthology to be particularly vulnerable to the vicissitudes of time: love can alter, and its subjects thus feel with a heightened vividness the pains of mutability and mortality which affect all human beings. Byron's Haidée and Shakespeare's Juliet manifest and articulate the fragility and vulnerability of young love with particular poignancy and delicacy. Crabbe's widow suggests that amatory passion may, indeed, be altogether inimical to enduringly satisfactory relations between man and woman. Pope's Clarissa reminds her friends that youthful flirtatiousness and beauty must mature into something deeper if a woman is to preserve any respect and sanity in later life.

Throughout the anthology, love is seen as a greater power than that of the individual (usually male) figures who arouse the passions and desires of the heroines. Shakespeare's Venus, the goddess of love herself, appeals to the universal beneficence of her power (as manifested in the attraction of Adonis' horse to a young mare in heat), but simultaneously displays its more disturbing aspect in her impotent passion for the stubbornly resistant boy. Her frustrations are in keeping with the spirit of the whole collection, which, in its cumulative implications, is decidedly anti-utopian, and suggests that there are no easy or comprehensive solutions to the difficulties and pains of human existence – of which the condition of love offers an exemplary instance. The 'mutuality' which is sometimes offered as an ideal to which human relations should aspire, is seen, in this anthology, as a seldom-attainable ideal. In his 'Franklin's Tale', Chaucer recognizes that love can never be sustained by the dominance of one party over the other:

> Love will not be constrained by mastery;
> When mastery cometh, the God of Love anon
> Beateth his wings, and, farewell, he is gone!

But Chaucer's own narratives show that love-relationships without some attempt at 'mastery' are rare. And he and his fellow poets indicate that other human qualities – good humour, forbearance and forgiveness – must counterbalance overwhelming desire, if relations between lovers are to achieve even a temporary stability. For Milton, full mutuality between human partners was only achievable during the blessed short period before the Fall. Shelley could only imagine such a union in a mysterious realm of Platonic ideals beyond everyday words and experience. The passion of love, this collection suggests, is a phenomenon in which, as in life itself, pleasures are inextricably linked with pains, and which requires tolerance and endurance, sometimes of a heroic nature, from those experiencing its power.

Note on Texts and Annotation

Since this anthology is designed for the general reader, texts are presented in as accessible a form as possible, with the minimum of editorial apparatus. Spelling and punctuation are modernized and normalized, even in the cases of Chaucer and Spenser. The end-notes (keyed to the separate line-numbering of each extract) are designed to explain those words, phrases and references which are most likely to puzzle modern readers. Brief headnotes provide concise indications of the context and subject-matter of each extract, but no attempt has been made to summarize the longer narratives from which many of the extracts are taken – for which readers should consult the standard reference books.

We would like to thank Tom Mason and Myra Stokes for their advice during the preparation of this anthology, and to dedicate the collection to Kate and James, our daughter and son.

Women in Love:

Heroines in Verse

Andromache

Andromache, fearful of her husband Hector's fate, attempts to dissuade him from re-entering the battle before the walls of Troy.

'Too daring prince! Ah, whither dost thou run?
Ah too forgetful of thy wife and son!
And think'st thou not how wretched we shall be,
A widow I, an helpless orphan he!
For sure such courage length of life denies,   5
And thou must fall, thy virtue's sacrifice.
Greece in her single heroes strove in vain;
Now hosts oppose thee, and thou must be slain!
Oh grant me, gods, ere Hector meets his doom,
All I can ask of heaven, an early tomb!   10
So shall my days in one sad tenor run,
And end with sorrows as they first begun.
No parent now remains my griefs to share,
No father's aid, no mother's tender care.
The fierce Achilles wrapped our walls in fire,   15
Laid Thebè waste, and slew my warlike sire!
His fate compassion in the victor bred;
Stern as he was, he yet revered the dead,
His radiant arms preserved from hostile spoil,
And laid him decent on the funeral pile;   20
Then raised a mountain where his bones were burned,
The mountain nymphs the rural tomb adorned,
Jove's sylvan daughters bade their elms bestow
A barren shade, and in his honour grow.
          By the same arm my seven brave brothers fell,   25
In one sad day beheld the gates of hell,
While the fat herds and snowy flocks they fed,
Amid their fields the hapless heroes bled!
My mother lived to bear the victor's bands,
The queen of Hippoplacia's sylvan lands;   30
Redeemed too late, she scarce beheld again
Her pleasing empire and her native plain,

When, ah, oppressed by life-consuming woe,
She fell a victim to Diana's bow.
   Yet while my Hector still survives, I see 35
My father, mother, brethren, all, in thee.
Alas! my parents, brothers, kindred, all,
Once more will perish if my Hector fall.
Thy wife, thy infant, in thy danger share:
Oh prove a husband's and a father's care! 40
That quarter most the skilful Greeks annoy,
Where yon wild fig trees join the wall of Troy:
Thou, from this tower defend th' important post;
There Agamemnon points his dreadful host,
That pass Tydides, Ajax strive to gain, 45
And there the vengeful Spartan fires his train.
Thrice our bold foes the fierce attack have given,
Or led by hopes, or dictated from heaven.
Let others in the field their arms employ,
But stay my Hector here, and guard his Troy.' 50
   The chief replied, 'That post shall be my care,
Not that alone, but all the works of war.
How would the sons of Troy, in arms renowned,
And Troy's proud dames whose garments sweep the ground
Attaint the lustre of my former name, 55
Should Hector basely quit the field of fame?
My early youth was bred to martial pains,
My soul impels me to th' embattled plains;
Let me be foremost to defend the throne,
And guard my father's glories, and my own. 60
   Yet come it will, the day decreed by fates –
How my heart trembles while my tongue relates! –
The day when thou, imperial Troy, must bend,
And see thy warriors fall, thy glories end!
And yet no dire presage so wounds my mind, 65
My mother's death, the ruin of my kind,
Not Priam's hoary hairs defiled with gore,
Not all my brothers gasping on the shore,
As thine, Andromache, thy griefs I dread;
I see thee trembling, weeping, captive led! 70
In Argive looms our battles to design,
And woes, of which so large a part was thine!
To bear the victor's hard commands, or bring

The weight of waters from Hyperia's spring.
There, while you groan beneath the load of life,   75
They cry, "Behold the mighty Hector's wife!"
Some haughty Greek, who lives thy tears to see,
Embitters all thy woes by naming me.
The thoughts of glory past, and present shame,
A thousand griefs shall waken at the name!   80
May I lie cold before that dreadful day,
Pressed with a load of monumental clay!
Thy Hector, wrapped in everlasting sleep,
Shall neither hear thee sigh, nor see thee weep.'

Alexander Pope (1688–1744), translated from
Homer's *Iliad*, Book VI

Arabella

(1)

*Arabella, a clergyman's virtuous and learned daughter, sets
high standards for her future husband.*

Men she avoided; not in childish fear,
As if she thought some savage foe was near;
Not as a prude, who hides that man should seek,
Or who by silence hints that they should speak;
But with discretion all the sex she viewed,   5
Ere yet engaged, pursuing or pursued;
Ere love had made her to his vices blind,
Or hid the favourite's failings from her mind.
    Thus was the picture of the man portrayed,
By merit destined for so rare a maid;   10
At whose request she might exchange her state,
Or still be happy in a virgin's fate:
    He must be one with manners like her own,
His life unquestioned, his opinions known;
His stainless virtue must all tests endure,   15
His honour spotless, and his bosom pure;

She no allowance made for sex or times,
Of lax opinion – crimes were ever crimes;
No wretch forsaken must his frailty curse,
No spurious offspring drain his private purse.   20
He at all times his passions must command,
And yet possess – or be refused her hand.

(2)

Arabella rejects the suit of Edward Huntly.

    Then came a youth, and all their friends agreed,
That Edward Huntly was the man indeed;
Respectful duty he had paid awhile,
Then asked her hand, and had a gracious smile:
A lover now declared, he led the fair   5
To woods and fields, to visits, and to prayer;
Then whispered softly, 'Will you name the day?'
She softly whispered, 'If you love me, stay.'
'O try me not beyond my strength!' he cried;
'O be not weak!' the prudent Maid replied,   10
'But by some trial your affection prove:
Respect and not impatience argues love:
And love no more is by impatience known,
Than ocean's depth is by its tempests shown:
He whom a weak and fond impatience sways,   15
But for himself with all his fervour prays,
And not the maid he woos, but his own will obeys;
And will she love the being who prefers,
With so much ardour, his desire to hers?'
    Young Edward grieved, but let not grief be seen;   20
He knew obedience pleased his fancy's queen.
Awhile he waited, and then cried, 'Behold!
The year advancing, be no longer cold!'
For she had promised, 'Let the flowers appear,
And I will pass with thee the smiling year.'   25
Then pressing grew the youth; the more he pressed,
The less inclined the maid to his request.
'Let June arrive.' – Alas, when April came,
It brought a stranger, and the stranger, shame!
Nor could the lover from his house persuade   30

A stubborn lass whom he had mournful made.
Angry and weak, by thoughtless vengeance moved,
She told her story to the fair beloved;
In strongest words th' unwelcome truth was shown,
To blight his prospects, careless of her own.   35
          Our heroine grieved, but had too firm a heart
For him to soften, when she swore to part.
In vain his seeming penitence and prayer,
His vows, his tears; she left him in despair;
His mother fondly laid her grief aside,   40
And to the reason of the nymph applied:
     'It well becomes thee, lady, to appear,
But not to be, in very truth, severe.
Although the crime be odious in thy sight,
That daring sex is taught such things to slight.   45
His heart is thine, although it once was frail;
Think of his grief, and let his love prevail!'
     'Plead thou no more,' the lofty lass returned;
'Forgiving woman is deceived and spurned.
Say that the crime is common – shall I take   50
A common man my wedded lord to make?
See, a weak woman by his arts betrayed,
An infant born his father to upbraid!
Shall I forgive his vileness, take his name,
Sanction his error, and partake his shame?   55
No! this assent would kindred frailty prove;
A love for him would be a vicious love.
Can a chaste maiden secret counsel hold
With one whose crime by every mouth is told?
Forbid it spirit, prudence, virtuous pride;   60
He must despise me, were he not denied;
The way from vice the erring mind to win
Is with presuming sinners to begin,
And show, by scorning them, a just contempt for sin.'

          George Crabbe (1754–1832), from 'Arabella'

Ariadne

Ariadne laments her desertion by Theseus, whom she has helped to
escape from the Labyrinth, on the island of Naxos.

Theseus, O Theseus, hark! but yet in vain
   Alas, deserted, I complain!
It was some neighbouring rock, more soft than he,
   Whose hollow bowels pitied me,
And, beating back that false and cruel name,   5
   Did comfort and revenge my flame.
   Then, faithless, whither wilt thou fly?
   Stones dare not harbour cruelty.

Tell me you gods, whoe'er you are,
Why, O why, made you him so fair?   10
   And tell me, wretch, why thou
   Mad'st not thyself more true?
Beauty from him may copies take,
And more majestic heroes make,
   And falsehood learn a wile,   15
   From him, too, to beguile.
     Restore my clew;
     'Tis here most due,
For 'tis a labyrinth of more subtle art
To have so fair a face, so foul a heart.   20

The ravenous vulture tear his breast,
The rolling stone disturb his rest;
     Let him next feel
     Ixion's wheel,
    And add one fable more   25
    To cursing poets' store;
And then – yet rather let him live, and twine
His woof of days with some thread stol'n from mine;
But if you'll torture him, howe'er,
Torture my heart, you'll find him there.   30

    Till my eyes drank up his,
     And his drank mine,
    I ne'er thought souls might kiss
     And spirits join;

                    Pictures till then   35
              Took me as much as men,
                    Nature and art
              Moving alike my heart;
        But his fair visage made me find
                    Pleasures and fears,   40
                    Hopes, sighs, and tears,
        As several seasons of the mind.
              Should thine eye, Venus, on his dwell,
              Thou would'st invite him to thy shell,
              And, caught by that live jet,   45
              Venture the second net,
        And, after all thy dangers, faithless he,
        Should'st thou but slumber, would forsake ev'n thee.

William Cartwright (1611–43), from 'Ariadne
deserted by Theseus, as she sits upon a rock in
the island of Naxos, thus complains'

Asia

*Asia, Prometheus' wife, responds to his voice, heard on the air,
and affirms their spiritual reunion in a diviner realm.*

              My soul is an enchanted boat,
                 Which, like a sleeping swan, doth float
              Upon the silver waves of thy sweet singing;
                 And thine doth like an angel sit
                 Beside a helm conducting it,   5
              Whilst all the winds with melody are ringing.
                 It seems to float ever, for ever,
                 Upon that many-winding river,
                 Between mountains, woods, abysses,
                 A paradise of wildernesses!   10
              Till, like one in slumber bound,
        Borne to the ocean, I float down, around,
Into a sea profound, of ever-spreading sound.

Meanwhile thy spirit lifts its pinions
In music's most serene dominions,   15
Catching the winds that fan that happy
          heaven.
And we sail on, away, afar,
Without a course, without a star,
But by the instinct of sweet music driven;
Till through Elysian garden islets   20
By thee, most beautiful of pilots,
Where never mortal pinnace glided,
The boat of my desire is guided:
Realms where the air we breathe is love,
Which in the winds and on the waves doth
                    move,   25
Harmonizing this earth with what we feel above.

We have passed Age's icy caves,
And Manhood's dark and tossing waves,
And Youth's smooth ocean, smiling to betray:
Beyond the glassy gulfs we flee   30
Of shadow-peopled Infancy,
Through Death and Birth, to a diviner day;
A paradise of vaulted bowers,
Lit by downward-gazing flowers,
And watery paths that wind between 35
Wildernesses calm and green,
Peopled by shapes too bright to see,
And rest, having beheld – somewhat like thee –
Which walk upon the sea, and chant melodiously!

Percy Bysshe Shelley (1792–1822), from
Prometheus Unbound, Act II

Aurora Leigh

(1)

The poet Aurora Leigh rejects a proposal of marriage from her
cousin, the philanthropist Romney Leigh.

'What you love
Is not a woman, Romney, but a cause:
You want a helpmate, not a mistress, sir,
A wife to help your ends, – in her no end.
Your cause is noble, your ends excellent,   5
But I, being most unworthy of these and that,
Do otherwise conceive of love. Farewell.'
'Farewell, Aurora? You reject me thus?'
He said.
　　　'Sir, you were married long ago.
You have a wife already whom you love,   10
Your social theory. Bless you both, I say.
For my part, I am scarcely meek enough
To be the handmaid of a lawful spouse.
Do I look a Hagar, think you?'
　　　　　　　　'So you jest.'
'Nay, so, I speak in earnest,' I replied.   15
'You treat of marriage too much like, at least,
A chief apostle: you would bear with you
A wife ... a sister ... shall we speak it out?
A sister of charity.'
　　　　　　　'Then, must it be
Indeed farewell? And was I so far wrong   20
In hope and in illusion, when I took
The woman to be nobler than the man,
Yourself the noblest woman, in the use
And comprehension of what love is, – love,
That generates the likeness of itself   25
Through all heroic duties? so far wrong,
In saying bluntly, venturing truth on love,
"Come, human creature, love and work with me," –
Instead of "Lady, thou art wondrous fair,
And, where the Graces walk before, the Muse   30

Will follow at the lightning of their eyes,
And where the Muse walks, lovers need to creep:
Turn round and love me, or I die of love." '
      With quiet indignation I broke in:
'You misconceive the question like a man,   35
Who sees a woman as the complement
Of his sex merely. You forget too much
That every creature, female as the male,
Stands single in responsible act and thought
As also in birth and death. Whoever says   40
To a loyal woman, "Love and work with me,"
Will get fair answers if the work and love,
Being good themselves, are good for her – the best
She was born for. Women of a softer mood,
Surprised by men when scarcely awake to life,   45
Will sometimes only hear the first word, love,
And catch up with it any kind of work,
Indifferent, so that dear love go with it.
I do not blame such women, though, for love,
They pick much oakum; earth's fanatics make   50
Too frequently heaven's saints. But *me* your work
Is not the best for, – nor your love the best,
Nor able to commend the kind of work
For love's sake merely. Ah, you force me, sir,
To be overbold in speaking of myself: 55
I too have my vocation, – work to do,
The heavens and earth have set me since I changed
My father's face for theirs, and, though your world
Were twice as wretched as you represent,
Most serious work, most necessary work   60
As any of the economists'. Reform,
Make trade a Christian possibility,
And individual right no general wrong;
Wipe out earth's furrows of the Thine and Mine,
And leave one green for men to play at bowls,   65
With innings for them all! ... What then, indeed,
If mortals are not greater by the head
Than any of their prosperities? What then,
Unless the artist keep up open roads
Betwixt the seen and unseen, – bursting through   70
The best of your conventions with his best,

The speakable, imaginable best
God bids him speak, to prove what lies beyond
Both speech and imagination? A starved man
Exceeds a fat beast: we'll not barter, sir,   75
The beautiful for barley. – And, even so,
I hold you will not compass your poor ends
Of barley-feeding and material ease,
Without a poet's individualism
To work your universal. It takes a soul,   80
To move a body: it takes a high-souled man,
To move the masses, even to a cleaner stye.
It takes the ideal, to blow a hair's-breadth off
The dust of the actual. – Ah, your Fouriers failed,
Because not poets enough to understand   85
That life develops from within. – For me,
Perhaps I am not worthy, as you say,
Of work like this: perhaps a woman's soul
Aspires, and not creates: yet we aspire,
And yet I'll try out your perhapses, sir,   90
And if I fail . . . why, burn me up my straw
Like other false works – I'll not ask for grace.
Your scorn is better, cousin Romney. I
Who love my art, would never wish it lower
To suit my stature. I may love my art.   95
You'll grant that even a woman may love art,
Seeing that to waste true love on anything
Is womanly, past question.'

(2)

*Aurora finally acknowledges her love for Romney, who is now
blind, and accepts him.*

'Passioned to exalt
The artist's instinct in me at the cost
Of putting down the woman's, I forgot
No perfect artist is developed here
From any imperfect woman. Flower from root,   5
And spiritual from natural, grade by grade
In all our life. A handful of the earth
To make God's image! the despised poor earth,

The healthy, odorous earth, – I missed with it
The divine Breath that blows the nostrils out   10
To ineffable inflatus, – ay, the breath
Which love is. Art is much, but Love is more.
O Art, my Art, thou'rt much, but Love is more!
Art symbolises heaven, but Love is God
And makes heaven. I, Aurora, fell from mine.   15
I would not be a woman like the rest,
A simple woman who believes in love
And owns the right of love because she loves,
And, hearing she's beloved, is satisfied
With what contents God. I must analyse,   20
Confront, and question, just as if a fly
Refused to warm itself in any sun
Till such was *in Leone*: I must fret,
Forsooth, because the month was only May,
Be faithless of the kind of proffered love,   25
And captious, lest it miss my dignity,
And scornful, that my lover sought a wife
To use ... to use! O Romney, O my love,
I am changed since then, changed wholly, – for indeed
If now you'd stoop so low to take my love   30
And use it roughly, without stint or spare,
As men use common things with more behind
(And, in this, ever would be more behind)
To any mean and ordinary end, –
The joy would set me like a star, in heaven,   35
So high up, I should shine because of height
And not of virtue. Yet in one respect,
Just one, beloved, I am in nowise changed:
I love you, loved you ... loved you first and last,
And love you on for ever. Now I know   40
I loved you always, Romney.'

Elizabeth Barrett Browning (1806–61), from
Aurora Leigh, Books II and IX

Belinda

Belinda, a young society belle, flirts with all the young men around her.

Not with more glories, in th' etherial plain,
The sun first rises o'er the purpled main,
Than, issuing forth, the rival of his beams
Launched on the bosom of the silver Thames.
Fair nymphs and well-dressed youths around her shone,   5
But every eye was fixed on her alone.
On her white breast a sparkling cross she wore,
Which Jews might kiss, and infidels adore.
Her lively looks a sprightly mind disclose,
Quick as her eyes, and as unfixed as those: 10
Favours to none, to all she smiles extends;
Oft she rejects, but never once offends.
Bright as the sun her eyes the gazers strike,
And, like the sun, they shine on all alike.
Yet graceful ease, and sweetness void of pride   15
Might hide her faults, if belles had faults to hide:
If to her share some female errors fall,
Look on her face, and you'll forget 'em all.

Alexander Pope (1688–1744), from
The Rape of the Lock, Canto II

Britomart

Britomart, the daughter of King Ryence of Britain, sees Arthegall's image in a magic mirror, and falls in love with him.

One day it fortunèd fair Britomart
Into her father's closet to repair;
For nothing he from her reserved apart,
Being his only daughter and his heir;
Where when she had espied that mirror fair, 5

Herself awhile therein she viewed in vain;
Though her avizing of the virtues rare
Which thereof spoken were, she gan again
Her to bethink of that might to herself pertain.

But as it falleth, in the gentlest hearts   10
Imperious Love hath highest set his throne,
And tyrannizeth in the bitter smarts
Of them, that to him buxom are and prone:
So thought this maid (as maidens use to done)
Whom fortune for her husband would allot,   15
Not that she lusted after any one;
For she was pure from blame of sinful blot,
Yet wist her life at last must link in that same knot.

Eftsoons there was presented to her eye
A comely knight, all armed in cómplete wise,   20
Through whose bright ventayle lifted up on high
His manly face, that did his foes agrize
And friends to terms of gentle truce entice,
Looked forth, as Phoebus' face out of the east
Betwixt two shady mountains doth arise;   25
Portly his person was, and much increased
Through his heroic grace and honourable gest.

His crest was covered with a couchant hound,
And all his armour seemed of antique mould,
But wondrous massy and assurèd sound,   30
And round about yfretted all with gold,
In which there written was with ciphers old,
'Achilles' arms, which Arthegall did win'.
And on his shield enveloped sevenfold
He bore a crownèd little ermilin,   35
That decked the azure field with her fair pouldred skin.

The damsel well did view his personage,
And likèd well, ne further fastened not,
But went her way; ne her unguilty age
Did ween, unwares, that her unlucky lot   40
Lay hidden in the bottom of the pot;
Of hurt unwist most danger doth redound:
But the false archer, which that arrow shot

So slyly that she did not feel the wound,
Did smile full smoothly at her weetless woeful stound.   45

    Thenceforth the feather in her lofty crest,
    Ruffèd of love, gan lowly to avail,
    And her proud portance and her princely gest,
    With which she erst triumphèd, now did quail:
    Sad, solemn, sour, and full of fancies frail   50
    She wox; yet wist she neither how, nor why;
    She wist not, silly maid, what she did ail,
    Yet wist she was not well at ease perdy,
Yet thought it was not love, but some meláncholy.

    So soon as Night had with her pallid hue   55
    Defaced the beauty of the shining sky,
    And reft from men the world's desirèd view,
    She with her nurse adown to sleep did lie;
    But sleep full far away from her did fly:
    Instead thereof sad sighs, and sorrows deep   60
    Kept watch and ward about her warily,
    That nought she did but wail, and often steep
Her dainty couch with tears which closely she did weep.

    And if that any drop of slumbering rest
    Did chance to still into her weary sprite,   65
    When feeble nature felt herself oppressed,
    Straightway with dreams, and with fantastic sight
    Of dreadful things, the same was put to flight;
    That oft out of her bed she did astart,
    As one with view of ghastly fiends affright: 70
    Tho gan she to renew her former smart,
And think of that fair visage written in her heart.

Edmund Spenser (*c.* 1552–99), from *The Fairy Queen*, Book III

Circe

Circe, the island enchantress who turns men into beasts, longs for a true lover.

Where is my love? Does someone cry for me
Not knowing whom he calls? Does his soul cry
For mine to grow beside it, grow in it?
Does he beseech the gods to give him me,
The one unknown rare woman by whose side   5
No other woman thrice as beautiful
Could once seem fair to him; to whose voice heard
In any common tones no sweetest sound
Of love made melody on silver lutes,
Or singing like Apollo's when the gods   10
Grow pale with happy listening, might be peered
For making music to him; whom once found
There will be no more seeking anything?
            Oh love, oh love, oh love, art not yet come
Out of the waiting shadows into life?   15
Art not yet come after so many years
That I have longed for thee? Come! I am here.
            Not yet. For surely I should feel a sound
Of his far answer if now in the world
He sought me who will seek me – Oh, ye gods,   20
Will he not seek me? Is all a dream?
Will there be only these, these bestial things
Who wallow in their styes, or mop and mow
Among the trees, or munch in pens and byres,
Or snarl and filch behind their wattled coops;   25
These things who had believed that they were men?
            Nay, but he *will* come. Why am I so fair,
And marvellously minded, and with sight
Which flashes suddenly on hidden things,
As the gods see, who do not need to look?   30
Why wear I in my eyes that stronger power
Than basilisks, whose gaze can only kill,
To draw men's souls to me to live or die
As I would have them? Why am I given pride
Which yet longs to be broken, and this scorn,   35

Cruel and vengeful, for the lesser men
Who meet the smiles I waste for lack of him,
And grow too glad? Why am I who I am?
But for the sake of him whom fate will send
One day to be my master utterly,   40
That he should take me, the desire of all,
Whom only he in the world could bow to him.
        Oh, sunlike glory of pale glittering hairs,
Bright as the filmy wires my weavers take
To make me golden gauzes – Oh, deep eyes,   45
Darker and softer than the bluest dusk
Of august violets, darker and deep
Like crystal fathomless lakes in summer noons –
Oh, sad sweet longing smile – Oh, lips that tempt
My very self to kisses – oh, round cheeks   50
Tenderly radiant with the even flush
Of pale smoothed coral – perfect lovely face
Answering my gaze from out this fleckless pool –
Wonder of glossy shoulders, chiselled limbs –
Should I be so your lover as I am,   55
Drinking an exquisite joy to watch you thus
In all a hundred changes through the day,
But that I love you for him till he comes,
But that my beauty means his loving it?

                    Augusta Webster (1837–94), from 'Circe'

Clarissa

*After Belinda's hysterical reaction to the loss of her lock of hair,
her friend Clarissa commends the virtues of 'good humour'.*

        'Say why are beauties praised and honoured most,
The wise man's passion, and the vain man's toast?
Why decked with all that land and sea afford,
Why angels called, and angel-like adored?
Why round our coaches crowd the white-gloved beaus,   5
Why bows the side-box from its inmost rows?

How vain are all these glories, all our pains,
Unless good sense preserve what beauty gains:
That men may say, when we the front-box grace,
"Behold the first in virtue, as in face!"   10
Oh! if to dance all night, and dress all day,
Charmed the smallpox, or chased old age away;
Who would not scorn what housewife's cares produce,
Or who would learn one earthly thing of use?
To patch, nay ogle, might become a saint,   15
Nor could it sure be such a sin to paint.
But since, alas, frail beauty must decay,
Curled or uncurled, since locks will turn to grey;
Since painted, or not painted, all shall fade,
And she who scorns a man must die a maid;   20
What then remains but well our power to use,
And keep good humour still whate'er we lose?
And trust me, dear, good humour can prevail,
When airs, and flights, and screams, and scolding fail.
Beauties in vain their pretty eyes may roll;   25
Charms strike the sight, but merit wins the soul.'

Alexander Pope (1688–1744), from
The Rape of the Lock, Canto V

Cleopatra

(1)

Cleopatra thinks of Antony and her former Roman lovers.

O Charmian!
Where think'st thou he is now? Stands he, or sits he?
Or does he walk? Or is he on his horse?
O happy horse, to bear the weight of Antony!
Do bravely, horse! for wot'st thou whom thou mov'st?   5
The demi-Atlas of this earth, the arm
And burgonet of men. He's speaking now,
Or murmuring, 'Where's my serpent of old Nile?'

For so he calls me. Now I feed myself
With most delicious poison. Think on me,   10
That am with Phoebus' amorous pinches black,
And wrinkled deep in time. Broad-fronted Caesar,
When thou wast here above the ground, I was
A morsel for a monarch, and great Pompey
Would stand and make his eyes grow in my brow;   15
There would he anchor his aspect and die
With looking on his life.

(2)

Cleopatra tells Dolabella of her dream of Antony.

CLEOPATRA: I dreamed there was an Emperor Antony:
  Oh, such another sleep, that I might see
  But such another man!
DOLABELLA: If it might please ye, –
CLEOPATRA: His face was as the heavens; and therein stuck
  A sun and moon, which kept their course, and lighted   5
  The little O, the earth.
DOLABELLA: Most sovereign creature, –
CLEOPATRA: His legs bestrid the ocean; his reared arm
  Crested the world; his voice was propertied
  As all the tunèd spheres, and that to friends;
  But when he meant to quail and shake the orb,   10
  He was as rattling thunder. For his bounty,
  There was no winter in 't; an autumn 'twas
  That grew the more by reaping; his delights
  Were dolphin-like: they showed his back above
  The element they lived in; in his livery   15
  Walked crowns and crownets; realms and islands were
  As plates dropped from his pocket.
DOLABELLA: Cleopatra!
CLEOPATRA: Think you there was, or might be, such a man
  As this I dreamed of?
DOLABELLA: Gentle madam, no.
CLEOPATRA: You lie, up to the hearing of the gods.   20
  But, if there be, or ever were, one such,
  It's past the size of dreaming: nature wants stuff
  To vie strange forms with fancy; yet, to imagine

An Antony were nature's piece 'gainst fancy,
Condemning shadows quite.
DOLABELLA: Hear me, good madam.   25
   Your loss is as yourself, great; and you bear it
   As answering to the weight: would I might never
   O'ertake pursued success, but I do feel,
   By the rebound of yours, a grief that smites
   My very heart at root.   30

(3)

Cleopatra addresses Antony as she goes to her death.

CLEOPATRA: Give me my robe, put on my crown; I have
   Immortal longings in me: now no more
   The juice of Egypt's grape shall moist this lip:
   Yare, yare, good Iras; quick. Methinks I hear
   Antony call; I see him rouse himself   5
   To praise my noble act; I hear him mock
   The luck of Caesar, which the gods give men
   T' excuse their after wrath: husband, I come:
   Now to that name my courage prove my title!
   I am fire and air; my other elements   10
   I give to baser life. So; have you done?
   Come then, and take the last warmth of my lips.
   Farewell, kind Charmian; Iras, long farewell.
         [*Kisses them. Iras falls and dies.*]
   Have I the aspic in my lips? Dost fall?
   If thou and nature can so gently part,   15
   The stroke of death is as a lover's pinch,
   Which hurts, and is desired. Dost thou lie still?
   If thus thou vanishest, thou tell'st the world
   It is not worth leave-taking.
CHARMIAN: Dissolve, thick cloud, and rain; that I may say,   20
   The gods themselves do weep!
CLEOPATRA: This proves me base:
   If she first meet the curlèd Antony,
   He'll make demand of her, and spend that kiss
   Which is my heaven to have. Come, thou mortal wretch,
        [*To the asp, which she applies to her breast*]
   With thy sharp teeth this knot intrinsicate   25

Of life at once untie: poor venomous fool
Be angry, and dispatch. Oh, couldst thou speak,
That I might hear thee call great Caesar ass
Unpolicied!
CHARMIAN: O eastern star!
CLEOPATRA: Peace, peace!
Dost thou not see my baby at my breast,   30
That sucks the nurse asleep?
CHARMIAN: Oh break! Oh break!
CLEOPATRA: As sweet as balm, as soft as air, as gentle, –
O Antony! – Nay, I will take thee too.
          [*Applying another asp to her arm*]
What should I stay – [*Dies*]
CHARMIAN: In this vile world? So, fare thee well.
Now boast thee, Death, in thy possession lies   35
A lass unparalleled. Downy windows, close;
And golden Phoebus never be beheld
Of eyes again so royal! Your crown's awry;
I'll mend it, and then play.

William Shakespeare (1564–1616), from
Antony and Cleopatra, Acts I and V

Criseyde

(1)

*Criseyde expresses her feelings about Troilus, whose suit has been
pressed by her uncle, Pandarus.*

She thoughtë well that Troïlus' persón
She knew by sight and eek his gentilesse,
And thus she said, 'All were it nought to done,
To grant him love, yet, for his worthiness,
It were honóur with play and with gladness   5
In honesty with such a lord to deal,
For mine estate, and also for his heal.

Eek well wot I my Kingë's son is he;
And since he hath to see me such delight,
If I would utterly his sightë flee,   10
Paraunter he might have me in despite,
Through which I mightë stand in worsë plight;
Now were I wise me hatë to purchase,
Withouten need, there I may stand in grace?

In everything, I wot, there lieth measúre.   15
For though a man forbedë drunkenness,
He nought forbet that every creäture
Be drinkëless for alway, as I guess;
Eek, since I wot for me is his distress,
I n' oughtë not for that thing him despise,   20
Since it is so, he meaneth in good wise.

And eek I know, of longë time agone,
His thewës good, and that he is not nice.
N' avauntour, saith men, certain is he none;
Too wise is he to do so great a vice;   25
Ne als I nil him never so cherísh,
That he may make avaunt, by justë cause;
He shall me never bind in such a clause.

Now set a case, the hardest is, ywis,
Men mightë deemë that he loveth me: 30
What dishonóur were it untó me, this?
May I him let of that? Why nay, pardee!
I know alsó, and all day hear and see,
Men loven women all beside their leave,
And when them list no morë, let them leave.   35

I think, eek, how he able is for to have
Of all this noble town the thriftiest,
To be his love, so she her honour save;
For out and out he is the worthiest,
Save only Hector, which that is the best.   40
And yet his life all lieth now in my cure;
But such is love, and eek my áventure.

Ne me to love, a wonder is it nought;
For well wot I myself, so God me speed
(All would I that no man wist of this thought),   45

I am one the fairestë, out of dread,
And goodliestë, who that taketh heed;
And so men say in all the town of Troy.
What wonder is though he of me have joy?

I am mine ownë woman, well at ease,   50
I thank it God – as after mine estate;
Right young, and stand untied in lusty lease,
Withouten jealousy or such debate;
Shall noon husbandë say to me 'checkmate!'
For either they be full of jealousy,   55
Or masterful, or lovë novelry.

What shall I do? To what fine live I thus?
Shal I not love, in case if that me lest?
What, pardee, I am not religïous!
And though that I my heartë set at rest   60
Upon this knight, that is the worthiest,
And keep alway my honour and my name,
By allë right, it may do me no shame.'

(2)

*After the consummation of their love, Criseyde declares her
devotion to Troilus.*

To that Criseydë answered right anon,
And with a sigh she said, 'O heartë dear,
The game, ywis, so far forth now is gone,
That first shall Phoebus fallë from his sphere,
And every eagle been the dovë's fere,   5
And every rock out of his placë start,
Ere Troïlus out of Criseydë's heart!

Ye be so deep in-with my heartë grave,
That, though I would it turn out of my thought,
As wisely very God my soulë save,   10
To diën in the pain, I couldë nought!
And, for the love of God that us hath wrought,
Let in your brain none other fantasy
So creepë, that it causë me to die!

And that ye me would have as fast in mind   15
As I have you, that would I you beseech;
And, if I wistë soothly that to find,
God mightë not a point my joyës eech!
But, heartë mine, withouten morë speech,
Beth to me true, or ellës were it ruth;   20
For I am thine, by God and by my troth!

Beth glad forthy, and live in sickerness;
Thus said I ne'er ere this, ne shall to mo;
And if to you it were a great gladness
To turn again, soon after that ye go,   25
As fain would I as ye that it were so,
As wisely God mine heartë bring to rest!'
And him in armës took, and oftë kissed.

(3)

Criseyde expresses her feelings about forsaking Troilus for Diomede.

But truëly, the story telleth us,
There madë never woman morë woe
Than she, when that she falsëd Troïlus.
She said, 'Alas, for now is clean ago
My name of truth in love, for evermo!   5
For I have falsëd one the gentilest
That ever was, and one the worthiest!

Alas, of me unto the worldë's end
Shall neither be ywritten nor ysung
No good word, for these bookës will me shend.   10
O, rollëd shall I be on many a tongue;
Throughout the world my bellë shall be rung;
And women most will hatë me of all.
Alas, that such a case me shouldë fall!

They will say, inasmuch as in me is,   15
I have them done dishonour, weylaway!
All be I not the first that did amiss,
What helpeth that to do my blame away?
But since I see there is no better way,
And that too late is now for me to rue,   20
To Diomede algate I will be true.

But, Troïlus, since I no better may,
And since that thus departen ye and I,
Yet pray I God, so give you right good-day
As for the gentilestë, truëly,   25
That e'er I saw, to servë faithfully,
And best can aye his lady honour keep.' –
And with that word she burst anon to weep.

'And certes, you ne hatë shall I never,
And friendë's love, that shall ye have of me,   30
And my good word, all should I liven ever.
And, truëly, I wouldë sorry be
For to see you in adversity.
And guiltëless, I wot well, I you leave;
But all shall pass; and thus take I my leave.'   35

But truëly, how long it was between,
That she forsook him for this Diomede,
There is no author telleth it, I ween.
Take every man now to his bookës heed:
He shal no termë finden, out of dread.   40
For though that he began to woo her soon,
Ere he her won, yet was there more to doon.

Ne me ne list this sely woman chide
Further than the story will devise.
Her name, alas, is publishëd so wide,   45
That for her guilt it ought enough suffice.
And if I might excuse her any wise,
For she so sorry was for her untruth,
Ywis, I would excuse her yet for ruth.

Geoffrey Chaucer (*c.* 1343–1400), from
Troilus and Criseyde, Books II, III and V

Dalilah

Dalilah protests that her betrayal of Samson to the Philistines was prompted by love.

And what if love, which thou interpret'st hate,
The jealousy of love, powerful of sway
In human hearts, nor less in mine towards thee,
Caused what I did? I saw thee mutable
Of fancy, feared lest one day thou wouldst leave me   5
As her at Timna, sought by all means therefore
How to endear, and hold thee to me firmest:
No better way I saw than by importuning
To learn thy secrets, get into my power
Thy key of strength and safety: thou wilt say;   10
Why then revealed? I was assured by those
Who tempted me, that nothing was designed
Against thee but safe custody, and hold:
That made for me, I knew that liberty
Would draw thee forth to perilous enterprises,   15
While I at home sat full of cares and fears
Wailing thy absence in my widowed bed;
Here I should still enjoy thee day and night
Mine and love's prisoner, not the Philistines',
Whole to myself, unhazarded abroad,   20
Fearless at home of partners in my love.
These reasons in love's law have passed for good,
Though fond and reasonless to some perhaps;
And love hath oft, well meaning, wrought much woe,
Yet always pity or pardon hath obtained.   25

John Milton (1608–74), from *Samson Agonistes*

Desdemona

Desdemona reaffirms her love for Othello in the face of his cruel jealousy.

                  O good Iago,
What shall I do to win my lord again?
Good friend, go to him; for, by this light of heaven,
I know not how I lost him. Here I kneel:
If e'er my will did trespass 'gainst his love,   5
Either in discourse of thought or actual deed,
Or that mine eyes, mine ears, or any sense,
Delighted them in any other form;
Or that I do not yet, and ever did,
And ever will – though he do shake me off   10
To beggarly divorcement – love him dearly,
Comfort forswear me! Unkindness may do much;
And his unkindness may defeat my life,
But never taint my love. I cannot say 'whore':
It does abhor me now I speak the word;   15
To do the act that might th' addition earn
Not the world's mass of vanity could make me.

    William Shakespeare (1564–1616), from *Othello*, Act IV

Dido

(1)

Dido declares her love for Aeneas who, voyaging to Italy, has been shipwrecked on the shores of Carthage.

    Speaks not Aeneas like a conqueror?
O blessèd tempests that did drive him in!
O happy sand that made him run aground!

Henceforth you shall be our Carthage gods!
Aye, but it may be he will leave my love,   5
And seek a foreign land called Italy.
O, that I had a charm to keep the winds
Within the closure of a golden ball,
Or that the Tyrrhene sea were in mine arms,
That he might suffer shipwreck on my breast,   10
As oft as he attempts to hoist up sail!
I must prevent him: wishing will not serve.
Go, bid my nurse take young Ascanius,
And bear him in the country to her house,
Aeneas will not go without his son: 15
Yet, lest he should – for I am full of fear –
Bring me his oars, his tackling, and his sails.
What if I sink his ships? O, he'll frown!
Better he frown than I should die for grief;
I cannot see him frown – it may not be!   20
Armies of foes resolved to win this town,
Or impious traitors vowed to have my life
Affright me not; only Aeneas' frown
Is that which terrifies poor Dido's heart:
Not bloody spears appearing in the air,   25
Presage the downfall of my empery,
Nor blazing comets threatens Dido's death;
It is Aeneas' frown that ends my days:
If he forsake me not, I never die,
For in his looks I see eternity,   30
And he'll make me immortal with a kiss.

Christopher Marlowe (1564–93), from
The Tragedy of Dido

(2)

*When Dido hears that Aeneas is intending to leave Carthage, she
upbraids him for his treachery and ingratitude, and prophesies that
her shade will haunt him.*

'False as thou art, and, more than false, foresworn!
Not sprung from noble blood, nor goddess-born,
But hewn from hardened entrails of a rock,
And rough Hyrcanian tigers gave thee suck!

Why should I fawn, what have I worse to fear?   5
Did he once look, or lent a listening ear,
Sighed when I sobbed, or shed one kindly tear?
All symptoms of a base ungrateful mind,
So foul that which is worse 'tis hard to find.
      Of man's injustice why should I complain?   10
The gods, and Jove himself, behold in vain
Triumphant treason, yet no thunder flies,
Nor Juno views my wrongs with equal eyes:
Faithless is earth, and faithless are the skies!
Justice is fled, and Truth is now no more!   15
      I saved the shipwrecked exile on my shore;
With needful food his hungry Trojans fed;
I took the traitor to my throne and bed:
Fool that I was – 'tis little to repeat
The rest – I stored and rigged his ruined fleet.   20
I rave! I rave! A god's command he pleads,
And makes heav'n áccessory to his deeds.
Now Lycian lots, and now the Delian god,
Now Hermes is employed from Jove's abode,
To warn him hence – as if the peaceful state   25
Of heavenly powers were touched with human fate!
      But go! Thy flight no longer I detain.
Go, seek thy promised kingdom through the main!
Yet if the heavens will hear my pious vow,
The faithless waves, not half so false as thou,   30
Or secret sands shall sepulchres afford
To thy proud vessels and their perjured lord.
Then shalt thou call on injured Dido's name:
Dido shall come, in a black sulph'ry flame,
When death has once dissolved her mortal frame;   35
Shall smile to see the traitor vainly weep;
Her angry ghost, arising from the deep,
Shall haunt thee waking, and disturb thy sleep.
At least my shade thy punishment shall know,
And Fame shall spread the pleasing news below.'   40

John Dryden (1631–1700), translated from
Virgil's *Aeneid*, Book IV

Dolly

Dolly, a milkmaid, is seduced at a country fair.

Ere the sun o'er the hills, round and red, 'gan a peeping,
    To beckon the chaps to their ploughs,
Too thinking and restless all night to be sleeping,
    I brushed off to milking my cows;
To get my jobs forward, and eager preparing   5
    To be off in time to the wake,
Where yielding so freely a kiss for a fairing,
    I made a most shocking mistake.

Young Ralph met me early, and off we were steering,
    I cuddled me close to his side;   10
The neighbours, while passing, my fondness kept jeering,
    'Young Ralph's timely suited!' they cried.
But he bid me mind not their evil pretensions,
    'Fools mun,' says he, 'talk for talk's sake;'
And, kissing me, 'Doll, if you've any 'prehensions,   15
    Let me tell you, my wench, you mistake.'

My cows when we passed them kept booing and mooing,
    In truth, but they made me to stare;
As much as to say, 'Well, now, Dolly, you're going,
    Mind how you get on at the fair.'   20
While bidden 'good speed' from each gazing beholder,
    'Good journey away to the wake,'
The mowers stopped whetting, to look o'er their shoulder,
    Saying 'Dolly, don't make a mistake.'

I couldn't but mind the fine morning so charming,   25
    The dew-drops they glittered like glass;
And all o'er the meads were the buttercups swarming,
    Like so many suns in the grass;
I thought as we passed them, if such a thing could be
    What a fine string of beads they would make;   30
But when I could think of such nonsense, it would be
    Because I had made no mistake.

So on his arm hanging, with stories beguiling,
    Of what he would buy me when there,

The road cutting short with his kissing and smiling,   35
      He 'veigled me off to the fair:
Such presents he proffered before I could claim 'em,
      To keep while I lived for his sake,
And what I liked best, o'er and o'er begged me name 'em,
      That he mightn't go make a mistake.   40

And, lud, what a crushing and crowding were wi' 'em,
      What noises are heard at a fair;
Here some sell so cheap, as they'd even go gi' 'em,
      If conscience would take, they declare:
Some so good, 'tis e'en worth more than money to buy 'em, 45
      Fine gingerbread nuts and plum-cake;
For truth they bid Ralph, ere he treated me, try 'em,
      And then there could be no mistake.

A sly Merry-Andrew was making his speeches,
      With chaps and girls round him a swarm,   50
And, 'Mind,' said he, fleering, 'ye chubby-faced witches,
      Your fairings don't do you some harm.'
The hay-cocks he named, in the meads passing by 'em,
      When weary we came from the wake,
So soft, so inviting, for rest we mun try 'em;   55
      What a fool should I be to mistake.

But promised so faithful, behaviour so clever,
      Such gifts as Ralph crammed in my hand,
How could I distrust of his goodness? O never!
      And who could his goodness withstand?   60
His ribbons, his fairings, past counting, or nearly,
      Some return when he pressed me to make,
Good manners mun give, while he loved me so dearly:
      Ah! where could I see the mistake?

Till dark night he kept me, with fussing and lying,   65
      How he'd see me safe home to my cot;
Poor maiden, so easy, so free in complying,
      I the showman's good caution forgot:
All the by-ways he led me, 'twas vain to dispute it,
      The moon blushed for shame, naughty rake!   70
Behind a cloud sneaking – but darkness well suited
      His baseness, who caused the mistake.

In vain do I beg him to wed and have done wi 't,
    So fair as he promised we should;
We couldn't do worse than as how we've begun wi 't,   75
    Let matters turn out as they would:
But he's always a talking 'bout wedding expenses,
    And the wages he's gotten to take;
Too plain can I see through his evil pretences,
    Too late I find out the mistake.   80

Oh, what mun I do with my mother reprovin',
    Since she will do nothing but chide?
For when old transgressors have been in the oven,
    They know where the young ones may hide.
In vain I seek pity with plaints and despairings,   85
    Always ding'd on the nose with the wake:
Young maidens! be cautious who give you your fairings;
    You see what attends a mistake.

John Clare (1793–1864), 'Dolly's Mistake; or
The Ways of the Wake'

The Duchess of Malfi

The Duchess declares her love for her steward Antonio.

DUCHESS: The misery of us that are born great!
    We are forced to woo, because none dare woo us:
    And as a tyrant doubles with his words,
    And fearfully equivocates, so we
    Are forced t' express our violent passions   5
    In riddles, and in dreams, and leave the path
    Of simple virtue, which was never made
    To seem the thing it is not: Go, go, brag
    You have left me heartless; mine is in your bosom;
    I hope 'twill multiply love there: you do tremble: 10
    Make not your heart so dead a piece of flesh,
    To fear more than to love me; sir, be confident:
    What is 't distracts you? This is flesh and blood, sir;

'Tis not the figure cut in alabaster
Kneels at my husband's tomb. Awake, awake, man, 15
I do here put off all vain ceremony,
And only do appear to you a young widow
That claims you for her husband, and like a widow,
I use but half a blush in 't.
ANTONIO: Truth speak for me,
I will remain the constant sanctuary 20
Of your good name.
DUCHESS: I thank you, gentle love,
And 'cause you shall not come to me in debt –
Being now my steward – here upon your lips
I sign your *quietus est*: this you should have begged now,
I have seen children oft eat sweetmeats thus, 25
As fearful to devour them too soon.

John Webster (*c.* 1578–*c.* 1632), from
The Duchess of Malfi, Act I

Elaine

Elaine, the Fair Maid of Astolat, falls in love with Lancelot, whom she has nursed after he was injured in a joust.

There morn by morn, arraying her sweet self
In that wherein she deemed she looked her best,
She came before Sir Lancelot, for she thought,
'If I be loved, these are my festal robes,
If not, the victim's flowers before he fall.' 5
And Lancelot ever pressed upon the maid
That she should ask some goodly gift of him
For her own self or hers: 'And do not shun
To speak the wish most near to your true heart;
Such service have ye done me, that I make 10
My will of yours, and Prince and Lord am I
In mine own land, and what I will I can.'
Then like a ghost she lifted up her face,

But like a ghost without the power to speak.
And Lancelot saw that she withheld her wish,   15
And bode among them yet a little space
Till he should learn it; and one morn it chanced
He found her in among the garden yews,
And said, 'Delay no longer, speak your wish,
Seeing I go today:' then out she brake: 20
'Going? and we shall never see you more.
And I must die for want of one bold word.'
'Speak: that I live to hear,' he said, 'is yours.'
Then suddenly and passionately she spoke:
'I have gone mad. I love you: let me die.'   25
'Ah, sister,' answered Lancelot, 'what is this?'
And innocently extending her white arms,
'Your love,' she said, 'your love – to be your wife.'
And Lancelot answered, 'Had I chosen to wed,
I had been wedded earlier, sweet Elaine: 30
But now there never will be wife of mine.'
'No, no,' she cried, 'I care not to be wife,
But to be with you still, to see your face,
To serve you, and to follow you through the world.'
And Lancelot answered, 'Nay, the world, the world,   35
All ear and eye, with such a stupid heart
To interpret ear and eye, and such a tongue
To blare its own interpretation – nay,
Full ill then should I quit your brother's love,
And your good father's kindness.' And she said,   40
'Not to be with you, not to see your face –
Alas for me then, my good days are done.'
'Nay, noble maid,' he answered, 'ten times nay!
This is not love: but love's first flash in youth,
Most common: yea, I know it of mine own self: 45
And you yourself will smile at your own self
Hereafter, when you yield your flower of life
To one more fitly yours, not thrice your age:
And then will I, for true you are and sweet
Beyond mine old belief in womanhood,   50
More specially should your good knight be poor,
Endow you with broad land and territory
Even to the half my realm beyond the seas,

So that would make you happy: furthermore,
Ev'n to the death, as though ye were my blood,   55
In all your quarrels will I be your knight.
This will I do, dear damsel, for your sake,
And more than this I cannot.'
                              While he spoke
She neither blushed nor shook, but deathly-pale
Stood grasping what was nearest, then replied: 60
'Of all this will I nothing;' and so fell,
And thus they bore her swooning to her tower.

Alfred, Lord Tennyson (1809–92), from
'Lancelot and Elaine'

Eloisa

*Eloisa, incarcerated in her convent, remembers her illicit love for
her teacher, Abelard, who has been castrated as a punishment for
their affair.*

Thou know'st how guiltless first I met thy flame,
When Love approached me under Friendship's name;
My fancy formed thee of angelic kind,
Some emanation of the all-beauteous mind.
Those smiling eyes, attempering every ray,   5
Shone sweetly lambent with celestial day.
Guiltless I gazed; heaven listened while you sung;
And truths divine came mended from that tongue.
From lips like those what precept failed to move?
Too soon they taught me 'twas no sin to love: 10
Back through the paths of pleasing sense I ran,
Nor wished an angel whom I loved a man.
Dim and remote the joys of saints I see,
Nor envy them that heaven I lose for thee.
How oft, when pressed to marriage, have I said,   15
Curse on all laws but those which love has made!
Love, free as air, at sight of human ties

Spreads his light wings, and in a moment flies.
Let wealth, let honour, wait the wedded dame,
August her deed, and sacred be her fame;   20
Before true passion all those views remove:
Fame, Wealth, and Honour, what are you to Love?
The jealous god, when we profane his fires,
Those restless passions in revenge inspires,
And bids them make mistaken mortals groan,   25
Who seek in love for aught but love alone.
Should at my feet the world's great master fall,
Himself, his throne, his world, I'd scorn 'em all:
Not Caesar's empress wou'd I deign to prove;
No, make me mistress to the man I love;   30
If there be yet another name more free,
More fond, than mistress, make me that to thee!
Oh happy state, when souls each other draw,
When love is liberty, and nature, law:
All then is full, possessing, and possessed,   35
No craving void left aching in the breast:
Ev'n thought meets thought, ere from the lips it part,
And each warm wish springs mutual from the heart.
This sure is bliss (if bliss on earth there be)
And once the lot of Abelard and me. [. . .]   40
      Come, Abelard, for what hast thou to dread?
The torch of Venus burns not for the dead.
Cut from the root my perished joys I see,
And love's warm tide for ever stopped in thee.
Nature stands checked; Religion disapproves;   45
Ev'n thou art cold – yet Eloïsa loves.
Ah hopeless, lasting flames, like those that burn
To light the dead, and warm th' unfruitful urn.
      What scenes appear where-e'er I turn my view,
The dear ideas, where I fly, pursue,   50
Rise in the grove, before the altar rise,
Stain all my soul, and wanton in my eyes.
I waste the matin lamp in sighs for thee,
Thy image steals between my God and me,
Thy voice I seem in every hymn to hear,   55
With every bead I drop too soft a tear.
When from the censer clouds of fragrance roll,

And swelling organs lift the rising soul,
One thought of thee puts all the pomp to flight,
Priests, tapers, temples, swim before my sight: 60
In seas of flame my plunging soul is drowned,
While altars blaze, and angels tremble round.
        While prostrate here in humble grief I lie,
Kind, virtuous drops just gathering in my eye,
While praying, trembling, in the dust I roll,   65
And dawning grace is opening on my soul:
Come, if thou dar'st, all charming as thou art!
Oppose thyself to heaven; dispute my heart;
Come, with one glance of those deluding eyes
Blot out each bright idea of the skies;   70
Take back that grace, those sorrows, and those tears;
Take back my fruitless penitence and prayers;
Snatch me, just mounting, from the blessed abode;
Assist the fiends, and tear me from my God!

Alexander Pope (1688–1744), from 'Eloisa to Abelard'

Emilia

Iago's wife Emilia reflects on the desires of husbands and wives.

But I do think it is their husbands' faults
If wives do fall: say that they slack their duties,
And pour our treasures into foreign laps,
Or else break out in peevish jealousies,
Throwing restraint upon us; or say they strike us,   5
Or scant our former having in despite;
Why, we have galls, and though we have some grace,
Yet have we some revenge. Let husbands know
Their wives have sense like them: they see and smell
And have their palates both for sweet and sour,   5
As husbands have. What is it that they do
When they change us for others? Is it sport?
I think it is; and doth affection breed it?
I think it doth; is't frailty that thus errs?

It is so too: and have not we affections,   15
Desires for sport, and frailty, as men have?
Then let them use us well: else let them know,
The ills we do, their ills instruct us so.

William Shakespeare (1564–1616), from *Othello*, Act IV

Erminia

*Erminia, a princess from Antioch, fears for the safety of the
crusader prince, Tancred, with whom she had previously fallen in
love while his prisoner. Tancred is now fighting in single combat
with the Saracen Argantes before the walls of Jerusalem.*

All long to see them end this doubtful fray,
And as they favour, so they wish success,
These hope true virtue shall obtain the day,
Those trust on fury, strength, and hardiness;
But on Erminia most this burden lay,   5
Whose looks her trouble and her fear express;
   For on this dangerous combat's doubtful end,
   Her joy, her comfort, hope, and life depend.

Her the sole daughter of that hapless king,
That of proud Antioch late wore the crown,   10
The Christian soldiers to Tancredi bring,
When they had sacked and spoiled that glorious town;
But he, in whom all good and virtue spring,
The virgin's honour saved, and her renown;
   And when her city and her state were lost,   15
   Then was her person loved and honoured most.

He honoured her, served her, and leave her gave,
And willed her go whither and when she list,
Her gold and jewels had he care to save,
And them restorèd all, she nothing missed.   20
She, that beheld this youth and person brave,
When, by this deed, his noble mind she wist,

Laid ope her heart for Cupid's shaft to hit,
Who never knots of love more surer knit.

Her body free, captivèd was her heart,   25
And love the keys did of that prison bear,
Prepared to go, it was the death to part
From that kind lord, and from that prison dear;
But thou, O honour, which esteemèd art
The chiefest vesture noble ladies wear,   30
      Enforcèd her against her will to wend
      To Aladine, her mother's dearest friend.

At Sion was this princess entertained
By that old tyrant and her mother dear,
Whose loss too soon the woeful damsel plained;   35
Her grief was such, she lived not half the year;
Yet banishment, nor loss of friends constrained
The hapless maid, her passion to forbear;
      For though exceeding were her woe and grief,
      Of all her sorrows yet her love were chief.   40

The sely maid in secret longing pined,
Her hope a mote drawn up by Phoebus' rays,
Her love a mountain seemed, whereon bright shined
Fresh memory of Tancred's worth and praise;
Within her closet if herself she shrined,   45
A hotter fire her tender heart assays;
      Tancred at last, to raise her hope nigh dead,
      Before these walls did his broad ensign spread.

The rest to view the Christian army feared,
Such seemed their number, such their power and might,   50
But she alone her troubled forehead cleared,
And on them spread her beauty shining bright;
In every squadron when it first appeared,
Her curious eye sought out her chosen knight;
      And every gallant that the rest excels,   55
      The same seems him, so love and fancy tells.

Within the kingly palace builded high,
A turret standeth near the city's wall,
From which Erminia might at ease descry
The western host, the plains and mountains all,   60
And there she stood all the long day to spy,
From Phoebus' rising to his evening fall,

And with her thoughts disputed of his praise,
And every thought a scalding sigh did raise.

From hence the furious combat she surveyed,   65
And felt her heart tremble with fear and pain,
Her secret thoughts thus to her fancy said,
'Behold thy dear in danger to be slain;'
So with suspect, with fear and grief dismayed,
Attended she her darling's loss or gain,   70
      And every when the Pagan lift his blade,
      The stroke a wound in her weak bosom made.

But when she saw the end, and wist withal
Their strong contention should eftsoons begin,
Amazement strange her courage did appal,   75
Her vital blood was icy cold within;
Sometimes she sighèd, sometimes tears let fall,
To witness what distress her heart was in;
      Hopeless, dismayed, pale, sad, astonishèd,
      Her love her fear, her fear her torment bred.   80

Her idle brain into her soul presented
Death, in an hundred ugly fashions painted,
And if she slept, then was her grief augmented,
With such sad visions were her thoughts acquainted;
She saw her lord with wounds and hurts tormented,   85
How he complained, called for her help, and fainted;
      And found, awaked from that unquiet sleeping,
      Her heart with panting sore; eyes red with weeping.

Yet these presages of his coming ill,
Not greater cause of her discomfort were;   90
She saw his blood from his deep wounds distil,
Nor what he suffered could she bide or bear;
Besides, report her longing ear did fill,
Doubling his danger, doubling so her fear,
      That she concludes – so was her courage lost –   95
      Her wounded lord was weak, faint, dead almost.

And for her mother had her taught before
The secret virtue of each herb that springs,
Beside fit charms for every wound or sore
Corruption breedeth, or misfortune brings   100
(An art esteemèd in those times of yore,

Beseeming daughters of great lords and kings),
        She would herself be surgeon of her knight,
        And heal him with her skill, or with her sight.

                        Edward Fairfax (d. 1635), translated from
                        Tasso's *Gerusalemme Liberata*, Book VI

Eve

(1)

Eve, speaking to Adam, recalls her first meeting with him.

        'That day I oft remember, when from sleep
        I first awaked, and found my self reposed
        Under a shade of flowers, much wondering where
        And what I was, whence thither brought, and how.
        Not distant far from thence a murmuring sound   5
        Of waters issued from a cave and spread
        Into a liquid plain, then stood unmoved,
        Pure as th' expanse of heaven; I thither went
        With unexperienced thought, and laid me down
        On the green bank, to look into the clear   10
        Smooth lake, that to me seemed another sky.
        As I bent down to look, just opposite,
        A shape within the watery gleam appeared
        Bending to look on me; I started back,
        It started back, but pleased I soon returned,   15
        Pleased it returned as soon with answering looks
        Of sympathy and love; there I had fixed
        Mine eyes till now, and pined with vain desire,
        Had not a voice thus warned me, "What thou seest,
        What there thou seest, fair creature, is thyself,   20
        With thee it came and goes: but follow me,
        And I will bring thee where no shadow stays
        Thy coming, and thy soft embraces, he
        Whose image thou art, him thou shall enjoy
        Inseparably thine, to him shalt bear   25

Multitudes like thyself, and thence be called
Mother of human race". What could I do,
But follow straight, invisibly thus led?
Till I espied thee, fair indeed and tall,
Under a platan, yet methought less fair,   30
Less winning soft, less amiably mild,
Than that smooth watery image; back I turned,
Thou following cried'st aloud, "Return, fair Eve,
Whom fliest thou? Whom thou fliest, of him thou art,
His flesh, his bone; to give thee being I lent   35
Out of my side to thee, nearest my heart
Substantial life, to have thee by my side
Henceforth an individual solace dear;
Part of my soul I seek thee, and thee claim
My other half." With that thy gentle hand   40
Seized mine; I yielded, and from that time see
How beauty is excelled by manly grace
And wisdom, which alone is truly fair.'

(2)

Eve celebrates her love for Adam.

'With thee conversing I forget all time,
All seasons and their change, all please alike.
Sweet is the breath of morn, her rising sweet,
With charm of earliest birds; pleasant the sun
When first on this delightful land he spreads   5
His orient beams, on herb, tree, fruit, and flower,
Glistering with dew; fragrant the fertile earth
After soft showers; and sweet the coming on
Of grateful evening mild, then silent night
With this her solemn bird and this fair moon,   10
And these the gems of heaven, her starry train:
But neither breath of morn when she ascends
With charm of earliest birds, nor rising sun
On this delightful land, nor herb, fruit, flower,
Glistering with dew, nor fragrance after showers,   15
Nor grateful evening mild, nor silent night
With this her solemn bird, nor walk by moon,
Or glittering starlight without thee is sweet.'

(3)

Eve expresses contrition for her part in the Fall.

'Forsake me not thus, Adam, witness heaven
What love sincere and reverence in my heart
I bear thee, and unweeting have offended,
Unhappily deceived; thy suppliant
I beg, and clasp thy knees; bereave me not,   5
Whereon I live, thy gentle looks, thy aid,
Thy counsel in this uttermost distress,
My only strength and stay: forlorn of thee,
Whither shall I betake me, where subsist?
While yet we live, scarce one short hour perhaps,   10
Between us two let there be peace, both joining,
As joined in injuries, one enmity
Against a foe by doom express assigned us,
That cruel serpent: on me exercise not
Thy hatred for this misery befallen,   15
On me already lost, me than thyself
More miserable; both have sinned, but thou
Against God only, I against God and thee,
And to the place of judgement will return,
There with my cries importune heaven, that all   20
The sentence from thy head removed may light
On me, sole cause to thee of all this woe,
Me, me only just object of his ire.'

John Milton (1608–74), from *Paradise Lost*,
Books IV and IX

Francesca da Rimini

Francesca tells of her illicit love for her brother-in-law, Paolo.

And then I turned unto their side my eyes,
        And said, 'Francesca, thy sad destinies
        Have made me sorrow till the tears arise.
But tell me, in the season of sweet sighs,

By what and how thy love to passion rose,   5
So as his dim desires to recognize?'
Then she to me: 'The greatest of all woes
    Is to remind us of our happy days
    In misery, and that thy teacher knows.
But if to learn our passion's first root preys   10
    Upon thy spirit with such sympathy,
    I will do even as he who weeps and says.
We read one day for pastime, seated nigh,
    Of Lancelot, how love enchained him too.
    We were alone, quite unsuspiciously.   15
But oft our eyes met, and our cheeks in hue
    All o'er discoloured by that reading were;
    But one point only wholly us o'erthrew;
When we read the long-sighed-for smile of her,
    To be thus kissed by such devoted lover,   20
    He, who from me can be divided ne'er,
Kissed my mouth, trembling in the act all over:
    Accursèd was the book and he who wrote!
    That day no further leaf we did uncover.'
While thus one spirit told us of their lot,   25
    The other wept, so that with pity's thralls
    I swooned, as if by death I had been smote,
And fell down even as a dead body falls.

George Gordon, Lord Byron (1788–1824),
translated from Dante's *Inferno*, Canto V

Griselda

*Griselda's husband has tested her by taking her two children and
by declaring his intention to remarry, and to return Griselda to
her father, and poverty. She responds.*

'But théreas ye me proffer such dowér
As I first brought, it is well in my mind
It were my wretched clothës, nothing fair,
The which to me were hard now for to find.

O goodë God, how gentle and how kind   5
Ye seemëd by your speech and your visage
The day that makëd was our marriage!

But sooth is said, algate I find it true –
For in effect it provëd is on me –
Love is not old as when that it is new.   10
But certes, lord, for none adversity,
To diën in the case, it shall not be
That e'er in word or work I shall repent
That I you gave mine heart in whole intent.

My lord, ye woot that, in my father's place,   15
Ye did me strip out of my poorë weed,
And richëly me cladden, of your grace.
To you brought I nought ellës, out of dread,
But faith and nakedness and maidenhead.
And here again my clothing I restore,   20
And eek my wedding ring, for evermore.

The remnant of your jewels ready be
Inwith your chamber, dare I safely sayn;
Naked out of my father's house,' quod she,
'I came, and naked must I turn again.   25
All your pleasancë will I foll'wen fain;
But yet I hope it be not your intent
That I smockléss out of your palace went.

Ye could nat do so dishonést a thing,
That thilkë womb in which your children lay   30
Shouldë, before the people, in my walking,
Be seen all barë; wherefore I you pray,
Let me not like a worm go by the way.
Remember you, mine ownë lord so dear,
I was your wife, though I unworthy were.   35

Wherfore, in guerdon of my maidenhead,
Which that I brought, and not again I bear,
As voucheth safe to give me, to my meed,
But such a smock as I was wont to wear,
That I therewith may wry the womb of her   40
That was your wife; and here take I my leave
Of you, mine ownë lord, lest I you grieve.'

'The smock,' quod he, 'that thou hast on thy
        back,
Let it be still, and bear it forth with thee.'
But well unnethës thilkë word he spake,   45
But went his way for ruth and for pitÿ.
Before the folk herselven strippeth she,
And in her smock, with head and foot all bare,
Toward her father's house forth is she fare.

Geoffrey Chaucer (*c.* 1343–1400), from
'The Clerk's Tale'

Guinevere

Guinevere reveals to Lancelot her jealousy of Elaine.

While thus he spoke, half turned away, the Queen
Brake from the vast oriel-embowering vine
Leaf after leaf, and tore, and cast them off,
Till all the place whereon she stood was green;
Then, when he ceased, in one cold passive hand   5
Received at once and laid aside the gems
There on a table near her, and replied:
    'It may be, I am quicker of belief
Than you believe me, Lancelot of the Lake.
Our bond is not the bond of man and wife.   10
This good is in it, whatsoe'er of ill,
It can be broken easier. I for you
This many a year have done despite and wrong
To one whom ever in my heart of hearts
I did acknowledge nobler. What are these?   15
Diamonds for me! They had been thrice their worth
Being your gift, had you not lost your own.
To loyal hearts the value of all gifts
Must vary as the giver's. Not for me!
For her! For your new fancy. Only this   20
Grant me, I pray you: have your joys apart.
I doubt not that however changed, you keep
So much of what is graceful: and myself
Would shun to break those bounds of courtesy

In which as Arthur's queen I move and rule: 25
So cannot speak my mind. An end to this!
A strange one! Yet I take it with Amen.
So pray you, add my diamonds to her pearls;
Deck her with these; tell her, she shines me down:
An armlet for an arm to which the Queen's   30
Is haggard, or a necklace for a neck
O as much fairer – as a faith once fair
Was richer than these diamonds – hers not mine –
Nay, by the mother of our Lord himself,
Or hers or mine, mine now to work my will –   35
She shall not have them.'
                 Saying which she seized,
And, through the casement standing wide for heat,
Flung them, and down they flashed, and smote the stream.
Then from the smitten surface flashed, as it were,
Diamonds to meet them, and they passed away.   40
Then while Sir Lancelot leant, in half-disdain
At love, life, all things, on the window ledge,
Close underneath his eyes, and right across
Where these had fallen, slowly passed the barge
Whereon the lily maid of Astolat   45
Lay smiling, like a star in blackest night.

Alfred, Lord Tennyson (1809–92), from 'Lancelot and Elaine'

Haidée

Haidée, a Greek pirate's daughter, falls in love with Don Juan, who has been shipwrecked on her island.

Haidée spoke not of scruples, asked no vows,
     Nor offered any; she had never heard
Of plight and promises to be a spouse,
     Or perils by a loving maid incurred;
She was all which pure ignorance allows,   5
     And flew to her young mate like a young bird;
And, never having dreamt of falsehood, she
Had not one word to say of constancy.

She loved, and was belovèd – she adored,
    And she was worshipped; after nature's fashion,   10
Their intense souls, into each other poured,
    If souls could die, had perished in that passion, –
But by degrees their senses were restored,
    Again to be o'ercome, again to dash on;
And, beating 'gainst his bosom, Haidée's heart   15
Felt as if never more to beat apart.

Alas! they were so young, so beautiful,
    So lonely, loving, helpless, and the hour
Was that in which the heart is always full,
    And, having o'er itself no further power,   20
Prompts deeds eternity can not annul,
    But pays off moments in an endless shower
Of hell-fire – all prepared for people giving
Pleasure or pain to one another living.

Alas, for Juan and Haidée! They were   25
    So loving and so lovely – till then never,
Excepting our first parents, such a pair
    Had run the risk of being damned for ever;
And Haidée, being devout as well as fair,
    Had, doubtless, heard about the Stygian river,   30
And hell and purgatory – but forgot
Just in the very crisis she should not.

They look upon each other, and their eyes
    Gleam in the moonlight; and her white arm clasps
Round Juan's head, and his around hers lies   35
    Half buried in the tresses which it grasps;
She sits upon his knee, and drinks his sighs,
    He hers, until they end in broken gasps;
And thus they form a group that's quite antique,
Half naked, loving, natural, and Greek.   40

And when those deep and burning moments passed,
    And Juan sunk to sleep within her arms,
She slept not, but all tenderly, though fast,
    Sustained his head upon her bosom's charms;
And now and then her eye to heaven is cast,   45
    And then on the pale cheek her breast now warms,

Pillowed on her o'erflowing heart, which pants
With all it granted, and with all it grants.

An infant when it gazes on a light,
      A child the moment when it drains the breast,   50
A devotee when soars the Host in sight,
      An Arab with a stranger for a guest,
A sailor when the prize has struck in fight,
      A miser filling his most hoarded chest,
Feel rapture; but not such true joy are reaping   55
As they who watch o'er what they love while sleeping.

For there it lies so tranquil, so beloved,
      All that it hath of life with us is living;
So gentle, stirless, helpless, and unmoved,
      And all unconscious of the joy 'tis giving;   60
All it hath felt, inflicted, passed, and proved,
      Hushed into depths beyond the watcher's diving;
There lies the thing we love with all its errors
And all its charms, like death without its terrors.

The lady watched her lover – and that hour   65
      Of Love's, and Night's, and Ocean's solitude,
O'erflowed her soul with their united power;
      Amidst the barren sand and rocks so rude
She and her wave-worn love had made their bower,
      Where nought upon their passion could intrude,   70
And all the stars that crowded the blue space
Saw nothing happier than her glowing face.

Alas, the love of women! It is known
      To be a lovely and a fearful thing;
For all of theirs upon that die is thrown,   75
      And if 'tis lost, life hath no more to bring
To them but mockeries of the past alone,
      And their revenge is as the tiger's spring,
Deadly, and quick, and crushing; yet, as real
Torture is theirs, what they inflict they feel.   80

They are right; for man, to man so oft unjust,
      Is always so to women; one sole bond
Awaits them, treachery is all their trust;
      Taught to conceal, their bursting hearts despond
Over their idol, till some wealthier lust   85

Buys them in marriage – and what rests beyond?
A thankless husband, next a faithless lover,
Then dressing, nursing, praying, and all's over.

Some take a lover, some take drams or prayers,
  Some mind their household, others dissipation,   90
Some run away, and but exchange their cares,
  Losing the advantage of a virtuous station;
Few changes e'er can better their affairs,
  Theirs being an unnatural situation,
From the dull palace to the dirty hovel: 95
Some play the devil, and then write a novel.

George Gordon, Lord Byron (1788–1824), from
Don Juan, Canto II

Helen of Troy

*Venus (in disguise) summons Helen to make love to Paris, whose
cowardice in battle she has just witnessed.*

She spoke, and Helen's secret soul was moved;
She scorned the champion, but the man she loved.
Fair Venus' neck, her eyes that sparkled fire,
And breast revealed the queen of soft desire.
Struck with her presence, straight the lively red   5
Forsook her cheek; and, trembling, thus she said:
'Then is it still thy pleasure to deceive?
And woman's frailty always to believe?
Say, to new nations must I cross the main,
Or carry wars to some soft Asian plain?   10
For whom must Helen break her second vow?
What other Paris is thy darling now?
Left to Atrides, victor in the strife,
An odious conquest and a captive wife,
Hence let me sail: and if thy Paris bear   15
My absence ill, let Venus ease his care.
A handmaid goddess at his side to wait,
Renounce the glories of thy heavenly state,

Be fixed for ever to the Trojan shore,
His spouse, or slave; and mount the skies no more.   20
For me, to lawless love no longer led,
I scorn the coward, and detest his bed;
Else should I merit everlasting shame,
And keen reproach, from every Phrygian dame:
Ill suits it now the joys of love to know,   25
Too deep my anguish, and too wild my woe.'
    Then thus, incensed, the Paphian queen replies:
'Obey the power from whom thy glories rise:
Should Venus leave thee, every charm must fly,
Fade from thy cheek, and languish in thy eye.   30
Cease to provoke me, lest I make thee more
The world's aversion, than their love before;
Now the bright prize for which mankind engage,
Then the sad victim of the public rage.'

Alexander Pope (1688–1744), translated from
Homer's *Iliad*, Book III

Helena

(1)

*Helena, despised by Demetrius, who loves Hermia in her stead,
reflects on the capriousness of love.*

How happy some o'er other some can be!
Through Athens I am thought as fair as she.
But what of that? Demetrius thinks not so;
He will not know what all but he do know:
And as he errs, doting on Hermia's eyes,   5
So I, admiring of his qualities.
Things base and vile, holding no quantity,
Love can transpose to form and dignity.
Love looks not with the eyes, but with the mind;
And therefore is winged Cupid painted blind: 10
Nor hath Love's mind of any judgement taste;

Wings and no eyes figure unheedy haste:
And therefore is Love said to be a child,
Because in choice he is so oft beguiled.
As waggish boys in game themselves forswear,   15
So the boy Love is perjured everywhere:
For ere Demetrius looked on Hermia's eyne,
He hailed down oaths that he was only mine;
And when this hail some heat from Hermia felt,
So he dissolved, and showers of oaths did melt.   20

(2)

Demetrius rejects Helena, who nevertheless begs for his love.

DEMETRIUS: Do I entice you? Do I speak you fair?
　　Or, rather, do I not in plainest truth
　　Tell you, I do not, nor I cannot love you?
HELENA: And ev'n for that do I love you the more.
　　I am your spaniel; and, Demetrius,   5
　　The more you beat me, I will fawn on you:
　　Use me but as your spaniel, spurn me, strike me,
　　Neglect me, lose me; only give me leave,
　　Unworthy as I am, to follow you.
　　What worser place can I beg in your love,   10
　　And yet a place of high respect with me,
　　Than to be usèd as you use your dog?
DEMETRIUS: Tempt not too much the hatred of my spirit;
　　For I am sick when I do look on thee.
HELENA: And I am sick when I look not on you.   15
DEMETRIUS: You do impeach your modesty too much,
　　To leave the city and commit yourself
　　Into the hands of one that loves you not;
　　To trust the opportunity of night
　　And the ill counsel of a desert place   20
　　With the rich worth of your virginity.
HELENA: Your virtue is my privilege: for that
　　It is not night when I do see your face,
　　Therefore I think I am not in the night;
　　Nor doth this wood lack worlds of company,   25
　　For you in my respect are all the world:
　　Then how can it be said I am alone,

When all the world is here to look on me?
DEMETRIUS: I'll run from thee and hide me in the brakes,
   And leave thee to the mercy of wild beasts.   30
HELENA: The wildest hath not such a heart as you.
   Run when you will, the story shall be changed:
   Apollo flies, and Daphne holds the chase;
   The dove pursues the griffin; the mild hind
   Makes speed to catch the tiger; bootless speed,   35
   When cowardice pursues and valour flies.
DEMETRIUS: I will not stay thy questions; let me go;
   Or, if thou follow me, do not believe
   But I shall do thee mischief in the wood.
HELENA: Ay, in the temple, in the town, the field,   40
   You do me mischief. Fie, Demetrius!
   Your wrongs do set a scandal on my sex:
   We cannot fight for love, as men may do;
   We should be wooed and were not made to woo.

William Shakespeare (1564–1616), from
A Midsummer Night's Dream, Acts I and II

Hero

(1)

Leander sees the priestess Hero officiating at the feast of Venus.
His love for her is secretly reciprocated.

And in the midst a silver altar stood,
There Hero sacrificing turtles' blood,
Veiled to the ground, veiling her eyelids close,
And modestly they opened as she rose.
Thence flew Love's arrow with the golden head,   5
And thus Leander was enamourèd.
Stone still he stood, and evermore he gazed,
Till with the fire that from his count'nance blazed,
Relenting Hero's gentle heart was strook;
Such force and virtue hath an amorous look.   10

It lies not in our power to love or hate,
For will in us is overruled by fate.
When two are stripped long ere the course begin,
We wish that one should lose, the other win.
And one especially do we affect,   15
Of two gold ingots like in each respect,
The reason no man knows, let it suffice,
What we behold is censured by our eyes.
Where both deliberate, the love is slight,
Who ever loved, that loved not at first sight?   20
        He kneeled, but unto her devoutly prayed;
Chaste Hero to herself thus softly said:
'Were I the saint he worships, I would hear him,'
And as she spake those words, came somewhat near him.
He started up, she blushed as one ashamed;   25
Wherewith Leander much more was inflamed.
He touched her hand, in touching it she trembled,
Love deeply grounded, hardly is dissembled,
These lovers parlèd by the touch of hands,
True love is mute, and oft amazed stands.   30

                              (2)

Hero repels Leander's advances, but nevertheless invites him to her
tower.

        Hero's looks yielded, but her words made war,
Women are won when they begin to jar.
Thus having swallowed Cupid's golden hook,
The more she strived, the deeper was she strook.
Yet ev'lly feigning anger, strove she still,   5
And would be thought to grant against her will.
So having paused awhile, at last she said:
'Who taught thee rhetoric to deceive a maid?
Aye me, such words as these should I abhor,
And yet I like them for the orator.'   10
        With that Leander stooped to have embraced her,
But from his spreading arms away she cast her,
And thus bespake him: 'Gentle youth, forbear
To touch the sacred garments which I wear.
Upon a rock, and underneath a hill,   15

Far from the town – where all is whist and still,
Save that the sea, playing on yellow sand,
Sends forth a rattling murmur to the land,
Whose sound allures the golden Morpheus,
In silence of the night to visit us –   20
My turret stands, and there God knows I play
With Venus' swans and sparrows all the day.
A dwarfish beldame bears me company,
That hops about the chamber where I lie,
And spends the night (that might be better spent)   25
In vain discourse and apish merriment.
Come thither'; as she spake this, her tongue tripped,
For unawares 'Come thither' from her slipped,
And suddenly her former colour changed,
And here and there her eyes through anger ranged.   30
And like a planet, moving several ways,
At one self-instant, she, poor soul, assays,
Loving, not to love at all, and every part
Strove to resist the motions of her heart.
And hands so pure, so innocent, nay such   35
As might have made heaven stoop to have a touch,
Did she uphold to Venus, and again
Vowed spotless chastity, but all in vain.
Cupid beats down her prayers with his wings,
Her vows above the empty air he flings: 40
All deep enraged, his sinewy bow he bent,
And shot a shaft that burning from him went,
Wherewith she, strooken, looked so dolefully,
As made Love sigh, to see his tyranny.
And as she wept, her tears to pearl he turned,   45
And wound them on his arm, and for her mourned.

Christopher Marlowe (1564–93), from *Hero and Leander*

Donna Julia

(1)

Donna Julia, a married lady of Seville, falls in love with the youthful Don Juan.

I can't tell whether Julia saw th' affair
    With other people's eyes, or if her own
Discoveries made, but none could be aware
    Of this, at least no symptom e'er was shown;
Perhaps she did not know, or did not care,   5
    Indifferent from the first, or callous grown:
I'm really puzzled what to think or say,
She kept her counsel in so close a way.

Juan she saw, and, as a pretty child,
    Caressed him often, such a thing might be   10
Quite innocently done, and harmless styled,
    When she had twenty years, and thirteen he;
But I am not so sure I should have smiled
    When he was sixteen, Julia twenty-three,
These few short years make wond'rous alterations,   15
Particularly amongst sun-burnt nations.

Whate'er the cause might be, they had become
    Changed; for the dame grew distant, the youth shy,
Their looks cast down, their greetings almost dumb,
    And much embarrassment in either eye;   20
There surely will be little doubt with some
    That Donna Julia knew the reason why,
But as for Juan, he had no more notion
Than he who never saw the sea of ocean.

Yet Julia's very coldness still was kind,   25
    And tremulously gentle her small hand
Withdrew itself from his, but left behind
    A little pressure, thrilling, and so bland
And slight, so very slight, that to the mind
    'Twas but a doubt; but ne'er magician's wand   30
Wrought change with all Armida's fairy art
Like what this light touch left on Juan's heart.

And if she met him, though she smiled no more,
     She looked a sadness sweeter than her smile,
As if her heart had deeper thoughts in store   35
     She must not own, but cherished more the while,
For that compression in its burning core;
     Ev'n innocence itself has many a wile,
And will not dare to trust itself with truth,
And love is taught hypocrisy from youth.   40

But passion most dissembles, yet betrays
     Ev'n by its darkness; as the blackest sky
Foretells the heaviest tempest, it displays
     Its workings through the vainly guarded eye,
And in whatever aspect it arrays   45
     Itself, 'tis still the same hypocrisy;
Coldness or anger, ev'n disdain or hate,
Are masks it often wears, and still too late.

Then there were sighs, the deeper for suppression,
     And stolen glances, sweeter for the theft,   50
And burning blushes, though for no transgression,
     Tremblings when met, and restlessness when left;
All these are little preludes to possession,
     Of which young passion cannot be bereft,
And merely tend to show how greatly love is   55
Embarrassed at first starting with a novice.

Poor Julia's heart was in an awkward state;
     She felt it going, and resolved to make
The noblest efforts for herself and mate,
     For honour's, pride's, religion's, virtue's sake;   60
Her resolutions were most truly great,
     And almost might have made a Tarquin quake;
She prayed the Virgin Mary for her grace,
As being the best judge of a lady's case.

She vowed she never would see Juan more,   65
     And next day paid a visit to his mother,
And looked extremely at the opening door,
     Which, by the Virgin's grace, let in another;
Grateful she was, and yet a little sore –
     Again it opens, it can be no other,   70
'Tis surely Juan now – No! I'm afraid
That night the Virgin was no further prayed.

She now determined that a virtuous woman
    Should rather face and overcome temptation,
That flight was base and dastardly, and no man   75
    Should ever give her heart the least sensation;
That is to say, a thought beyond the common
    Preference, that we must feel upon occasion,
For people who are pleasanter than others,
But then they only seem so many brothers.   80

And even if by chance – and who can tell?
    The devil's so very sly – she should discover
That all within was not so very well,
    And, if still free, that such or such a lover
Might please perhaps, a virtuous wife can quell   85
    Such thoughts, and be the better when they're over;
And if the man should ask, 'tis but denial:
I recommend young ladies to make trial.

And then there are such things as love divine,
    Bright and immaculate, unmixed and pure,   90
Such as the angels think so very fine,
    And matrons, who would be no less secure,
Platonic, perfect, 'just such love as mine':
    Thus Julia said – and thought so, to be sure,
And so I'd have her think, were I the man   95
On whom her reveries celestial ran.

Such love is innocent, and may exist
    Between young persons without any danger;
A hand may first, and then a lip be kissed;
    For my part, to such doings I'm a stranger,   100
But *hear* these freedoms form the utmost list
    Of all o'er which such love may be a ranger:
If people go beyond, 'tis quite a crime,
But not my fault – I tell them all in time.

Love, then, but love within its proper limits,   105
    Was Julia's innocent determination
In young Don Juan's favour, and to him its
    Exertion might be useful on occasion;
And, lighted at too pure a shrine to dim its
    Ethereal lustre, with what sweet persuasion   110

He might be taught, by love and her together –
I really don't know what, nor Julia either.

(2)

After the discovery of their affair, Donna Julia is committed to a
nunnery, and Don Juan is sent abroad. Before his departure, she
writes to him.

'They tell me 'tis decided you depart:
    'Tis wise – 'tis well, but not the less a pain;
I have no further claim on your young heart,
    Mine is the victim, and would be again;
To love too much has been the only art   5
    I used; – I write in haste, and if a stain
Be on this sheet, 'tis not what it appears,
My eyeballs burn and throb, but have no tears.

I loved, I love you; for this love have lost
    State, station, heaven, mankind's, my own esteem,   10
And yet cannot regret what it hath cost,
    So dear is still the memory of that dream;
Yet, if I name my guilt, 'tis not to boast,
    None can deem harshlier of me than I deem:
I trace this scrawl because I cannot rest –   15
I've nothing to reproach, or to request.

Man's love is of man's life a thing apart,
    'Tis woman's whole existence; man may range
The court, camp, church, the vessel, and the mart,
    Sword, gown, gain, glory, offer in exchange   20
Pride, fame, ambition, to fill up his heart,
    And few there are whom these cannot estrange;
Men have all these resources, we but one,
To love again, and be again undone.

You will proceed in pleasure, and in pride,   25
    Beloved and loving many; all is o'er
For me on earth, except some years to hide
    My shame and sorrow deep in my heart's core;
These I could bear, but cannot cast aside
    The passion which still rages as before,   30

And so farewell – forgive me, love me – No,
That word is idle now – but let it go.

My breast has been all weakness, is so yet;
      But still I think I can collect my mind;
My blood still rushes where my spirit's set,   35
      As roll the waves before the settled wind;
My heart is feminine, nor can forget –
      To all, except one image, madly blind;
So shakes the needle, and so stands the pole,
As víbrates my fond heart to my fixed soul.   40

I have no more to say, but linger still,
      And dare not set my seal upon this sheet,
And yet I may as well the task fulfil,
      My misery can scarce be more complete:
I had not lived till now, could sorrow kill;   45
      Death shuns the wretch who fain the blow would
          meet,
And I must ev'n survive this last adieu,
And bear with life, to love and pray for you!'

This note was written upon gilt-edged paper
      With a neat little crow-quill, slight and new;   50
Her small white hand could hardly reach the taper,
      It trembled as magnetic needles do,
And yet she did not let one tear escape her;
      The seal a sunflower; *'Elle vous suit partout,'*
The motto, cut upon a white cornelian;   55
The wax was superfine, its hue vermilion.

              George Gordon, Lord Byron (1788–1824), from
                        Don Juan, Canto I

Julia, daughter of Augustus

Julia, the Emperor Augustus' daughter, expresses her love for the poet Ovid, who has been banished from Rome because of his love for her.

Aye me, that virtue, whose brave eagle's wings
With every stroke blow stars in burning heaven;
Should like a swallow, preying toward storms,
Fly close to earth; and with an eager plume,
Pursue those objects which none else can see,   5
But seem to all the world the empty air.
Thus thou, poor Ovid, and all virtuous men,
Must prey like swallows on invisible food;
Pursuing flies, or nothing; and thus love,
And every worldly fancy, is transposed,   10
By worldly tyranny to what plight it list.
O father, since thou gav'st me not my mind,
Strive not to rule it: take but what thou gav'st
To thy disposure. Thy affections
Rule not in me; I must bear all my griefs;   15
Let me use all my pleasures: virtuous love
Was never scandal to a goddess' state.
But he's inflexible! and, my dear love,
Thy life may chance be shortened by the length
Of my unwilling speeches to depart.   20
Farewell, sweet life: though thou be yet exiled
Th' officious court, enjoy me amply still:
My soul, in this my breath, enters thine ears,
And on this turret's floor will I lie dead,
Till we may meet again. In this proud height,   25
I kneel beneath thee, in my prostrate love,
And kiss the happy sands that kiss thy feet.
Great Jove submits a sceptre to a cell;
And lovers, ere they part, will meet in hell.

Ben Jonson (1572/3–1637), from *Poetaster*, Act IV

Juliet

From her balcony, Juliet tempers Romeo's new-found passion with reason.

JULIET: By whose direction found'st thou out this place?
ROMEO: By Love, who first did prompt me to inquire;
    He lent me counsel and I lent him eyes.
    I am no pilot; yet, wert thou as far
    As that vast shore washed with the farthest sea,   5
    I would adventure for such merchandise.
JULIET: Thou know'st the mask of night is on my face,
    Else would a maiden blush bepaint my cheek
    For that which thou hast heard me speak tonight.
    Fain would I dwell on form, fain, fain deny   10
    What I have spoke: but farewell compliment!
    Dost thou love me? I know thou wilt say 'Ay',
    And I will take thy word: yet if thou swear'st,
    Thou mayst prove false; at lovers' perjuries
    They say Jove laughs. O gentle Romeo,   15
    If thou dost love, pronounce it faithfully:
    Or if thou think'st I am too quickly won,
    I'll frown and be perverse and say thee nay,
    So thou wilt woo; but else, not for the world.
    In truth, fair Montague, I am too fond,   20
    And therefore thou mayst think my 'haviour light:
    But trust me, gentleman, I'll prove more true
    Than those that have more cunning to be strange.
    I should have been more strange, I must confess,
    But that thou overheard'st, ere I was 'ware,   25
    My true love's passion: therefore pardon me,
    And not impute this yielding to light love,
    Which the dark night hath so discoverèd.
ROMEO: Lady, by yonder blessèd moon I swear
    That tips with silver all these fruit-tree tops, –   30
JULIET: O swear not by the moon, th' inconstant moon,
    That monthly changes in her circled orb,
    Lest that thy love prove likewise variable.
ROMEO: What shall I swear by?
JULIET: Do not swear at all;

Or, if thou wilt, swear by thy gracious self,   35
Which is the god of my idolatry,
And I'll believe thee.
ROMEO: If my heart's dear love –
JULIET: Well, do not swear: although I joy in thee,
    I have no joy of this contract tonight:
    It is too rash, too unadvised, too sudden;   40
    Too like the lightning which doth cease to be
    Ere one can say 'it lightens.' Sweet, good night!
    This bud of love, by summer's ripening breath,
    May prove a beauteous flower when next we meet.
    Good night, good night! As sweet repose and rest   45
    Come to thy heart as that within my breast!

William Shakespeare (1564–1616), from
Romeo and Juliet, Act II

Katharina

Katharina pleases her husband Petruchio by delivering an eloquent speech in praise of wifely duty, addressed to the peevish widow.

KATHARINA: Fie, fie! unknit that threatening unkind brow,
    And dart not scornful glances from those eyes,
    To wound thy lord, thy king, thy governor:
    It blots thy beauty as frosts do bite the meads,
    Confounds thy fame as whirlwinds shake fair buds,   5
    And in no sense is meet or amiable.
    A woman moved is like a fountain troubled,
    Muddy, ill-seeming, thick, bereft of beauty;
    And while it is so, none so dry or thirsty
    Will deign to sip or touch one drop of it.   10
    Thy husband is thy lord, thy life, thy keeper,
    Thy head, thy sovereign; one that cares for thee,
    And for thy maintenance commits his body
    To painful labour both by sea and land,
    To watch the night in storms, the day in cold,   15
    Whilst thou liest warm at home, secure and safe;

And craves no other tribute at thy hands
But love, fair looks and true obedience –
Too little payment for so great a debt.
Such duty as the subject owes the prince,   20
Ev'n such a woman oweth to her husband;
And when she's froward, peevish, sullen, sour,
And not obedient to his honest will,
What is she but a foul contending rebel
And graceless traitor to her loving lord?   25
I am ashamed that women are so simple
To offer war where they should kneel for peace;
Or seek for rule, supremacy and sway,
When they are bound to serve, love and obey.
Why are our bodies soft and weak and smooth,   30
Unapt to toil and trouble in the world,
But that our soft conditions and our hearts
Should well agree with our external parts?
Come, come, you froward and unable worms!
My mind hath been as big as one of yours,   35
My heart as great, my reason haply more,
To bandy word for word and frown for frown;
But now I see our lances are but straws,
Our strength as weak, our weakness past compare,
That seeming to be most which we indeed least are.   40
Then vail your stomachs, for it is no boot,
And place your hands below your husband's foot:
In token of which duty, if he please,
My hand is ready; may it do him ease.
PETRUCHIO: Why, there's a wench! Come on, and kiss me,
                                             Kate.   45

                            William Shakespeare (1564–1616), from
                            The Taming of the Shrew, Act V

A Lady (1)

A lady laments the absence of her lover at sea.

O happy dames, that may embrace
The fruit of your delight,
Help to bewail the woeful case
And eke the heavy plight
Of me, that wonted to rejoice   5
The fortune of my pleasant choice.
Good ladies, help to fill my mourning voice.

In ship, freight with rememberance
Of thoughts and pleasures past,
He sails that hath in governance   10
My life, while it will last;
With scalding sighs, for lack of gale,
Furthering his hope, that is his sail,
Toward me, the sweet port of his avail.

Alas, how oft in dreams I see   15
Those eyes that were my food,
Which sometime so delighted me
That yet they do me good;
Wherewith I wake with his return,
Whose absent flame did make me burn.   20
But when I find the lack, Lord, how I mourn!

When other lovers, in arms across,
Rejoice their chief delight,
Drownèd in tears, to mourn my loss,
I stand the bitter night   25
In my window, where I may see
Before the winds how the clouds flee.
Lo, what a mariner love hath made me!

And in green waves, when the salt flood
Doth rise by rage of wind,   30
A thousand fancies in that mood
Assail my restless mind.
Alas, now drencheth my sweet foe,
That with the spoil of my heart did go,
And left me; but, alas, why did he so!   35

And when the seas wax calm again,
To chase fro me annoy,
My doubtful hope doth cause me plain;
So dread cuts off my joy.
Thus is my wealth mingled with woe,   40
And of each thought a doubt doth grow:
Now he comes! Will he come? Alas, no, no!

Henry Howard, Earl of Surrey (?1517–47)

A Lady (2)

A lady laments her lost love.

I loved, I love, and when I love no more
Let joys and grief perish, and leave despair
To ring the knell of youth. He stood beside me,
The embodied vision of the brightest dream,
Which like a dawn heralds the day of life;   5
The shadow of his presence made my world
A Paradise. All familiar things he touched,
All common words he spoke, became to me
Like forms and sounds of a diviner world.
He was as is the sun in his fierce youth,   10
As terrible and lovely as a tempest;
He came, and went, and left me what I am.
Alas! Why must I think how oft we two
Have sat together near the river springs,
Under the green pavilion which the willow   15
Spreads on the floor of the unbroken fountain,
Strewn, by the nurslings that linger there,
Over that islet paved with flowers and moss,
While the musk-rose leaves, like flakes of crimson snow,
Showered on us, and the dove mourned in the pine,   20
Sad prophetess of sorrows not her own?
The crane returned to her unfrozen haunt,
And the false cuckoo bade the spray good morn;
And on a wintry bough the widowed bird,

Hid in the deepest night of ivy-leaves,   25
Renewed the vigils of a sleepless sorrow.
I, left like her, and leaving one like her,
Alike abandoned and abandoning
(Oh! unlike her in this!) the gentlest youth,
Whose love had made my sorrows dear to him,   30
Even as my sorrow made his love to me!

> Percy Bysshe Shelley (1792–1822), from
> 'Fragments of an Unfinished Drama'

A Lady (3)

A lady responds to a proposal lightly made and received.

1

'Yes,' I answered you last night;
  'No,' this morning, sir, I say:
Colours seen by candle-light
  Will not look the same by day.

2

When the viols played their best,   5
  Lamps above and laughs below,
Love me sounded like a jest,
  Fit for *yes* or fit for *no*.

3

Call me false or call me free,
  Vow, whatever light may shine, –   10
No man on your face shall see
  Any grief for change on mine.

4

Yet the sin is on us both;
  Time to dance is not to woo;
Wooing light makes fickle troth,   15
  Scorn of *me* recoils on *you*.

5

Learn to win a lady's faith
        Nobly, as the thing is high,
Bravely, as for life and death,
        With a loyal gravity.   20

6

Lead her from the festive boards,
        Point her to the starry skies;
Guard her, by your truthful words,
        Pure from courtship's flatteries.

7

By your truth she shall be true,   25
        Ever true, as wives of yore;
And her *yes*, once said to you,
        Shall be Yes for evermore.

Elizabeth Barrett Browning (1806–61),
'The Lady's "Yes" '

Lydia

Lydia, a society belle, expresses her jealousy of her young rival,
Chloe.

What shall I do? How spend the hateful day?
At chapel shall I wear the morn away?
Who there frequents at these unmodish hours,
But ancient matrons with their frizzled towers,
And grey religious maids? My presence there   5
Amid that sober train would own despair;
Nor am I yet so old; nor is my glance
As yet fixed wholly to devotion's trance.
        Straight then I'll dress, and take my wonted range
Through every Indian shop, through all the 'Change;   10
Where the tall jar erects his costly pride,

With antic shapes in China's azure dyed;
There careless lies the rich brocade unrolled,
Here shines a cabinet with burnished gold;
But then remembrance will my grief renew,   15
'Twas there the raffling dice false Damon threw;
The raffling dice to him decide the prize.
'Twas there he first conversed with Chloe's eyes;
Hence sprung th' ill-fated cause of all my smart,
To me the toy he gave, to her his heart.   20
But soon thy perj'ry in the gift was found,
The shivered china dropped upon the ground;
Sure omen that thy vows would faithless prove;
Frail was thy present, frailer is thy love.
   O happy Poll, in wiry prison pent;   25
Thou ne'er hast known what love or rivals meant,
And Pug with pleasure can his fetters bear,
Who ne'er believed the vows that lovers swear.
How am I cursed, unhappy and forlorn,
With perjury, with love, and rival's scorn!   30
False are the loose coquette's inveigling airs,
False is the pompous grief of youthful heirs,
False is the cringing courtier's plighted word,
False are the dice when gamesters stamp the board,
False is the sprightly widow's public tear;   35
Yet these to Damon's oaths are all sincere.
   Fly from perfidious man, the sex disdain;
Let servile Chloe wear the nuptial chain.
Damon is practised in the modish life,
Can hate, and yet be civil to a wife.   40
He games, he swears, he drinks, he fights, he roves,
Yet Chloe can believe he fondly loves.
Mistress and wife can well supply his need,
A miss for pleasure, and a wife for breed.
But Chloe's air is unconfined and gay,   45
And can perhaps an injured bed repay;
Perhaps her patient temper can behold
The rival of her love adorned with gold,
Powdered with diamonds; free from thought and care,
A husband's sullen humours she can bear.   50
   Why are these sobs? And why these streaming eyes?
Is love the cause? No, I the sex despise;

I hate, I loathe his base perfidious name.
Yet if he should but feign a rival flame?
But Chloe boasts and triumphs in my pains,   55
To her he's faithful, 'tis to me he feigns.

John Gay (1685–1732), from
'The Toilette: A Town Eclogue'

Madeline

Madeline awakens from her dream, to make love to Porphyro, who has come to her chamber secretly on St Agnes' Eve.

Awakening up, he took her hollow lute –
Tumultuous – and, in chords that tenderest be,
He played an ancient ditty, long since mute,
In Provence called 'La belle dame sans mercy':
Close to her ear touching the melody; –   5
Wherewith disturbed, she uttered a soft moan:
He ceased – she panted quick – and suddenly
Her blue affrayèd eyes wide open shone:
Upon his knees he sank, pale as smooth-sculptured stone.

Her eyes were open, but she still beheld,   10
Now wide awake, the vision of her sleep:
There was a painful change, that nigh expelled
The blisses of her dream so pure and deep
At which fair Madeline began to weep,
And moan forth witless words with many a sigh;   15
While still her gaze on Porphyro would keep;
Who knelt, with joinèd hands and piteous eye,
Fearing to move or speak, she looked so dreamingly.

'Ah, Porphyro!' said she, 'but even now
Thy voice was at sweet tremble in mine ear,   20
Made tuneable with every sweetest vow;
And those sad eyes were spiritual and clear:
How changed thou art! How pallid, chill, and drear!
Give me that voice again, my Porphyro,

Those looks immortal, those complainings dear!   25
    Oh leave me not in this eternal woe,
For if thou diest, my love, I know not where to go.'

Beyond a mortal man impassioned far
    At these voluptuous accents, he arose,
Ethereal, flushed, and like a throbbing star   30
    Seen 'mid the sapphire heaven's deep repose;
Into her dream he melted, as the rose
    Blendeth its odour with the violet, –
Solution sweet: meantime the frost-wind blows
    Like Love's alarum pattering the sharp sleet   35
Against the window-panes; St Agnes' moon hath set.

'Tis dark: quick pattereth the flaw-blown sleet:
    'This is no dream, my bride, my Madeline!'
'Tis dark: the icèd gusts still rave and beat:
    'No dream, alas! alas! and woe is mine!   40
Porphyro will leave me here to fade and pine. –
    Cruel! what traitor could thee hither bring?
I curse not, for my heart is lost in thine,
    Though thou forsakest a deceived thing; –
A dove forlorn and lost with sick unprunèd wing.' 45

'My Madeline! sweet dreamer! lovely bride!
    Say, may I be for aye thy vassal blest?
Thy beauty's shield, heart-shaped and vermeil dyed?
    Ah, silver shrine, here will I take my rest
After so many hours of toil and quest,   50
    A famished pilgrim, – saved by miracle.
Though I have found, I will not rob thy nest
    Saving of thy sweet self; if thou think'st well
To trust, fair Madeline, to no rude infidel.

Hark! 'tis an elfin-storm from faery land,   55
    Of haggard seeming, but a boon indeed:
Arise – arise! The morning is at hand; –
    The bloated wassaillers will never heed: –
Let us away, my love, with happy speed;
    There are no ears to hear, or eyes to see, –   60
Drowned all in Rhenish and the sleepy mead:
    Awake! arise! my love, and fearless be,
For o'er the southern moors I have a home for thee.'

John Keats (1795–1821), from 'The Eve of St Agnes'

Margaret

(1)

*The Wanderer retells Margaret's tale of the loss of her husband
Robert, a poor cottager.*

But, when I entered, Margaret looked at me
A little while; then turned her head away
Speechless, – and, sitting down upon a chair,
Wept bitterly. I wist not what to do,
Nor how to speak to her. Poor wretch, at last   5
She rose from off her seat, and then, 'O sir!' –
I cannot *tell* how she pronounced my name,
With fervent love, and with a face of grief
Unutterably helpless, and a look
That seemed to cling upon me – she enquired   10
If I had seen her husband. As she spake
A strange surprise and fear came to my heart,
Nor had I power to answer ere she told
That he had disappeared – not two months gone.
He left his house: two wretched days had passed,   15
And on the third, as wistfully she raised
Her head from off her pillow, to look forth,
Like one in trouble, for returning light,
Within her chamber-casement she espied
A folded paper, lying as if placed   20
To meet her waking eyes. This tremblingly
She opened – found no writing, but beheld
Pieces of money carefully enclosed,
Silver and gold. 'I shuddered at the sight,'
Said Margaret, 'for I knew it was his hand   25
That must have placed it there; and ere that day
Was ended, that long anxious day, I learned,
From one who by my husband had been sent
With the sad news, that he had joined a troop
Of soldiers, going to a distant land.   30
He left me thus – he could not gather heart
To take a farewell of me; for he feared

That I should follow with my babes, and sink
Beneath the misery of that wandering life.'

(2)

Margaret's decline in her husband's absence.

I found her sad and drooping: she had learned
No tidings of her husband; if he lived,
She knew not that he lived; if he were dead,
She knew not he was dead. She seemed the same
In person and appearance; but her house   5
Bespake a sleepy hand of negligence;
The floor was neither dry nor neat, the hearth
Was comfortless, and her small lot of books,
Which, in the cottage-window, heretofore
Had been piled up against the corner panes   10
In seemly order, now, with straggling leaves
Lay scattered here and there, open or shut,
As they had chanced to fall. Her infant babe
Had from its mother caught the trick of grief,
And sighed among its playthings. I withdrew,   15
And once again entering the garden saw,
More plainly still, that poverty and grief
Were now come nearer to her: weeds defaced
The hardened soil, and knots of withered grass:
No ridges there appeared of clear black mould,   20
No winter greenness; of her herbs and flowers,
It seemed the better part were gnawed away
Or trampled into earth; a chain of straw,
Which had been twined about the slender stem
Of a young apple-tree, lay at its root;   25
The bark was nibbled round by truant sheep.
Margaret stood near, her infant in her arms,
And, noting that my eye was on the tree,
She said, 'I fear it will be dead and gone
Ere Robert come again.' When to the house   30
We had returned together, she enquired
If I had any hope: but for her babe
And for her little orphan boy, she said,
She had no wish to live, that she must die

Of sorrow. Yet I saw the idle loom   35
Still in its place; his Sunday garments hung
Upon the self-same nail; his very staff
Stood undisturbed behind the door.

William Wordsworth (1770–1850), from
The Excursion, Book I

Mariana

Mariana, deserted by her lover, laments in her moated grange.

With blackest moss the flower-plots
    Were thickly crusted, one and all:
The rusted nails fell from the knots
    That held the pear to the gable-wall.
The broken sheds looked sad and strange: 5
    Unlifted was the clinking latch;
    Weeded and worn the ancient thatch
Upon the lonely moated grange.
        She only said, 'My life is dreary,
           He cometh not,' she said;   10
        She said, 'I am aweary, aweary,
           I would that I were dead!'

Her tears fell with the dews at even;
    Her tears fell ere the dews were dried;
She could not look on the sweet heaven,   15
    Either at morn or eventide.
After the flitting of the bats,
    When thickest dark did trance the sky,
    She drew her casement-curtain by,
And glanced athwart the glooming flats.   20
        She only said, 'The night is dreary,
           He cometh not,' she said;
        She said, 'I am aweary, aweary,
           I would that I were dead!'

Upon the middle of the night,   25

Waking she heard the night-fowl crow:
The cock sung out an hour ere light:
From the dark fen the oxen's low
Came to her: without hope of change,
In sleep she seemed to walk forlorn,   30
Till cold winds woke the gray-eyed morn
About the lonely moated grange.
She only said, 'The day is dreary,
He cometh not,' she said;
She said, 'I am aweary, aweary,   35
I would that I were dead!'

About a stone-cast from the wall
A sluice with blackened waters slept,
And o'er it many, round and small,
The clustered marish-mosses crept.   40
Hard by a poplar shook alway,
All silver-green with gnarlèd bark:
For leagues no other tree did mark
The level waste, the rounding gray.
She only said, 'My life is dreary,   45
He cometh not,' she said;
She said, 'I am aweary, aweary,
I would that I were dead!'

And ever when the moon was low,
And the shrill winds were up and away,   50
In the white curtain, to and fro,
She saw the gusty shadow sway.
But when the moon was very low,
And wild winds bound within their cell,
The shadow of the poplar fell   55
Upon her bed, across her brow.
She only said, 'The night is dreary,
He cometh not,' she said;
She said, 'I am aweary, aweary,
I would that I were dead!'   60

All day within the dreamy house,
The doors upon their hinges creaked;
The blue fly sung in the pane; the mouse
Behind the mouldering wainscot shrieked,
Or from the crevice peered about.   65

Old faces glimmered through the doors,
Old footsteps trod the upper floors,
Old voices called her from without.
      She only said, 'My life is dreary,
           He cometh not,' she said;   70
      She said, 'I am aweary, aweary,
           I would that I were dead!'

The sparrow's chirrup on the roof,
      The slow clock ticking, and the sound
Which to the wooing wind aloof   75
      The poplar made, did all confound
Her sense; but most she loathed the hour
      When the thick-moted sunbeam lay
      Athwart the chambers, and the day
Was sloping toward his western bower.   80
      Then said she, 'I am very dreary,
           He will not come,' she said;
      She wept, 'I am aweary, aweary,
           Oh God, that I were dead!'

Alfred, Lord Tennyson (1809–92), 'Mariana'

Medea

Medea is consumed with passion for Jason, who has come to her native Colchis in pursuit of the Golden Fleece, which is guarded by a watchful dragon. Her father Aeetes has set Jason impossible tasks: yoking to a plough a pair of fire-breathing bulls with bronze hooves, and sowing dragon's teeth from which armed men will arise.

     Meanwhile Medea, seized with fierce desire,
By reason strives to quench the raging fire,
But strives in vain! 'Some god,' she said, 'withstands,
And reason's baffled counsel countermands.
What unseen power does this disorder move?   5
'Tis Love – at least 'tis like what men call Love.
Else wherefore should the king's commands appear

To me too hard? But so, indeed, they are.
Why should I for a stranger fear, lest he
Should perish, whom I did but lately see?   10
His death or safety, what are they to me?
Wretch, from thy virgin-breast this flame expel,
And soon – Oh could I, all would then be well!
But Love, resistless Love, my soul invades;
Discretion this, affection that persuades.   15
I see the right, and I approve it too,
Condemn the wrong, and yet the wrong pursue.
Why, royal maid, should'st thou desire to wed
A wanderer, and court a foreign bed?
Thy native land, though barbarous, can present   20
A bridegroom worth a royal bride's consent:
And whether this adventurer lives or dies,
In Fate and Fortune's fickle pleasure lies.
Yet may he live, for to the powers above,
A virgin, led by no impulse of love,   25
So just a suit may for the guiltless move.
Whom would not Jason's valour, youth, and blood
Invite? Or, could these merits be withstood,
At least his charming person must incline
The hardest heart – I'm sure 'tis so with mine!   30
Yet, if I help him not, the flaming breath
Of bulls and earth-born foes must be his death.
Or, should he through these dangers force his way,
At last he must be made the dragon's prey.
If no remorse for such distress I feel,   35
I am a tigress, and my breast is steel.
Why do I scruple then to see him slain,
And with the tragic scene my eyes profane?
My magic's art employ, not to assuage
The savages, but t' enflame their rage?   40
His earth-born foes to fiercer fury move,
And áccessory to his murder prove?
The gods forbid! But prayers are idle breath,
When action only can prevent his death.
Shall I betray my father and the state,   45
To intercept a rambling hero's fate;
Who may sail off next hour, and saved from harms
By my assistance, bless another's arms?

Whilst I, not only of my hopes bereft,
But to unpitied punishment am left.   50
If he is false, let the ingrateful bleed!
But no such symptom in his looks I read.
Nature would ne'er have lavished so much grace
Upon his person, if his soul were base.
Besides, he first shall plight his faith, and swear   55
By all the gods; what therefore can'st thou fear?
Medea, haste, from danger set him free,
Jason shall thy eternal debtor be.'

Nahum Tate (1652–1715), translated from
Ovid's *Metamorphoses*, Book VII

Medora Trevilian

*Medora Trevilian begs her friend Araminta Vavasour to reject any
suitor who could not match the love they have shared.*

When I heard I was going abroad, love,
    I thought I was going to die;
We walked arm in arm to the road, love,
    We looked arm in arm to the sky;
And I said, 'When a foreign postilion   5
    Has hurried me off to the Po,
Forget not Medora Trevilian:
    My own Araminta, say "No!"'

We parted! but sympathy's fetters
    Reach far over valley and hill;   10
I muse o'er your exquisite letters,
    And feel that your heart is mine still;
And he who would share it with me, love, –
    The richest of treasures below, –
If he's not what Orlando should be, love,   15
    My own Araminta, say 'No!'

If he wears a top-boot in his wooing,
    If he comes to you riding a cob,
If he talks of his baking or brewing,
    If he puts up his feet on the hob,   20

If he ever drinks port after dinner,
      If his brow or his breeding is low,
If he calls himself 'Thompson' or 'Skinner,'
      My own Araminta, say 'No!'

If he studies the news in the papers   25
      While you are preparing the tea,
If he talks of the damps or the vapours
      While moonlight lies soft on the sea,
If he's sleepy while you are capricious,
      If he has not a musical 'Oh!'   30
If he does not call Werther delicious, –
      My own Araminta, say 'No!'

If he ever sets foot in the City
      Among the stockbrokers and Jews,
If he has not a heart full of pity,   35
      If he don't stand six feet in his shoes,
If his lips are not redder than roses,
      If his hands are not whiter than snow,
If he has not the model of noses, –
      My own Araminta say 'No!'   40

If he speaks of a tax or a duty,
      If he does not look grand on his knees,
If he's blind to a landscape of beauty,
      Hills, valleys, rocks, waters, and trees,
If he dotes not on desolate towers,   45
      If he likes not to hear the blast blow,
If he knows not the language of flowers, –
      My own Araminta, say 'No!'

He must walk – like a god of old story
      Come down from the home of his rest;   50
He must smile – like the sun in his glory
      On the buds he loves ever the best;
And oh! from its ivory portal
      Like music his soft speech must flow! –
If he speak, smile, or walk like a mortal,   55
      My own Araminta, say 'No!'

Don't listen to tales of his bounty,
      Don't hear what they say of his birth,
Don't look at his seat in the county,
      Don't calculate what he is worth;   60

But give him a theme to write verse on,
    And see if he turns out his toe;
If he's only an excellent person. –
    My own Araminta, say 'No!'

    Withrop Mackworth Praed (1802–39), from
'A Letter of Advice, from Miss Medora Trevilian at
   Padua, to Miss Araminta Vavasour, in London'

Monna Innominata

The unnamed lady writes of her love.

(1)

I dream of you to wake: would that I might
    Dream of you and not wake but slumber on;
    Nor find with dreams the dear companion gone,
As, summer ended, summer birds take flight.
In happy dreams I hold you full in sight,   5
    I blush again who waking look so wan;
    Brighter than sunniest day that ever shone,
In happy dreams your smile makes day of night.
Thus only in a dream we are at one,
    Thus only in a dream we give and take   10
        The faith that maketh rich who take or
            give;
    If thus to sleep is sweeter than to wake,
        To die were surely sweeter than to live,
Though there be nothing new beneath the sun.

(2)

Many in aftertimes will say of you
    'He loved her' – while of me what will they say?
    Not that I loved you more than just in play,
For fashion's sake as idle women do.
Even let them prate; who know not what we knew   5

Of love and parting in exceeding pain,
Of parting hopeless here to meet again,
Hopeless on earth, and heaven is out of view.
But by my heart of love laid bare to you,
     My love that you can make not void nor vain,   10
Love that foregoes you but to claim anew
Beyond this passage of the gate of death,
     I charge you at the Judgement make it plain
My love of you was life and not a breath.

     Christina Rossetti (1830–94), from *Monna Innominata*

Myrrha

*Myrrha, daughter of Cinyras, King of Cyprus, has been smitten
with an incestuous passion for her father. She meditates on her
plight.*

'Ah, Myrrha, whither would thy wishes tend?
Ye Gods, ye sacred laws, my soul defend
From such a crime as all mankind detest,
And never lodged before in human breast!
But is it sin? Or makes my mind alone   5
Th' imagined sin? For Nature makes it none.
What tyrant then these envious laws began,
Made not for any other beast but man!
The father-bull his daughter may bestride,
The horse may make his mother-mare a bride;   10
What piety forbids the lusty ram
Or more salacious goat to rut their dam?
The hen is free to wed the chick she bore,
And make a husband whom she hatched before.
All creatures else are of a happier kind,   15
Whom nor ill-natured laws from pleasure bind,
Nor thoughts of sin disturb their peace of mind.
     But man a slave of his own making lives;
The fool denies himself what Nature gives;
Too busy senates, with an over-care   20

To make us better than our kind can bear,
Have dashed a spice of envy in the laws,
And straining up too high have spoiled the cause.
Yet some wise nations break their cruel chains,
And own no laws, but those which love ordains;   25
Where happy daughters with their sires are joined,
And piety is doubly paid in kind.
O that I had been born in such a clime,
Not here, where 'tis the country makes the crime!
       But whither would my impious fancy stray?   30
Hence hopes, and ye forbidden thoughts, away!
His worth deserves to kindle my desires,
But with the love that daughters bear to sires.
Then had not Cinyras my father been,
What hindered Myrrha's hopes to be his queen?   35
But the perverseness of my fate is such,
That he's not mine because he's mine too much:
Our kindred-blood debars a better tie;
He might be nearer were he not so nigh.
Eyes and their objects never must unite,   40
Some distance is required to help the sight.
       Fain would I travel to some foreign shore,
Never to see my native country more,
So might I to myself myself restore;
So might my mind these impious thoughts remove,   45
And, ceasing to behold, might cease to love.
But stay I must, to feed my famished sight,
To talk, to kiss; and more, if more I might:
More, impious maid! What more canst thou design?
To make a monstrous mixture in thy line,   50
And break all statutes human and divine?
Canst thou be called, to save thy wretched life,
Thy mother's rival and thy father's wife?
Confound so many sacred names in one,
Thy brother's mother, sister to thy son!   55
And fear'st thou not to see th' infernal bands,
Their heads with snakes, with torches armed their hands,
Full at thy face th' avenging brands to bear,
And shake the serpents from their hissing hair?
But thou in time th' increasing ill control,   60
Nor first debauch the body by the soul;

Secure the sacred quiet of thy mind,
And keep the sanctions Nature has designed.'

John Dryden (1631–1700), translated from
Ovid's *Metamorphoses*, Book X

Ottima

*Ottima and her lover Sebald have murdered Ottima's husband,
Luca. When Sebald expresses remorse for the crime, Ottima
declares that she loves him better for it.*

OTTIMA: Well then, I love you better now than ever,
    And best (look at me while I speak to you) –
    Best for the crime; nor do I grieve, in truth,
    This mask, this simulated ignorance,
    This affectation of simplicity,   5
    Falls off our crime; this naked crime of ours
    May not be looked over: look it down!
    Great? let it be great; but the joys it brought,
    Pay they or no its price? Come: they or it!
    Speak not! The past, would you give up the past   10
    Such as it is, pleasure and crime together?
    Give up that noon I owned my love for you?
    The garden's silence: even the single bee
    Persisting in his toil, suddenly stopped,
    And where he hid you only could surmise   15
    By some campanula chalice set a-swing,
    Who stammered, 'Yes, I love you?'
SEBALD: And I drew
    Back; put far back your face with both my hands
    Lest you should grow too full of me – your face
    So seemed athirst for my whole soul and body!   20
OTTIMA: And when I ventured to receive you here,
    Made you steal hither in the mornings –
SEBALD: When
    I used to look up 'neath the shrub-house here,
    Till the red fire on its glazed windows spread

To a yellow haze?

OTTIMA: Ah – my sign was, the sun   25
Inflamed the sere side of yon chestnut-tree
Nipped by the first frost.

SEBALD: You would always laugh
At my wet boots: I had to stride thro' grass
Over my ankles.

OTTIMA: Then our crowning night!

SEBALD: The July night?

SEBALD: The day of it too, Sebald!   30
When heaven's pillars seemed o'erblowed with heat,
Its black-blue canopy suffered descend
Close on us both, to weigh down each to each,
And smother up all life except our life.
So lay we till the storm came.

SEBALD: How it came!   35

OTTIMA: Buried in woods we lay, you recollect:
Swift ran the searching tempest overhead;
And ever and anon some bright white shaft
Burned thro' the pine-tree roof, here burned and there.
As if God's messenger thro' the close wood screen   40
Plunged and replunged his weapon at a venture,
Feeling for guilty thee and me: then broke
The thunder like a whole sea overhead –

SEBALD: Yes!

OTTIMA: – While I stretched myself upon you, hands
To hands, my mouth to your hot mouth, and shook   45
All my locks loose, and covered you with them –
You, Sebald, the same you!

SEBALD: Slower, Ottima!

OTTIMA: And as we lay –

SEBALD: Less vehemently! Love me!
Forgive me! Take not words, mere words, to heart!
Your breath is worse than wine! Breathe slow, speak
                slow!   50
Do not lean on me!

OTTIMA: Sebald, as we lay,
Rising and falling only with our pants,
Who said, 'Let death come now! 'T is right to die!
Right to be punished! Nought completes such bliss

But woe!' Who said that?
SEBALD: How did we ever rise?   55
Was 't that we slept? Why did it end?
OTTIMA: I felt you
Taper into a point that ruffled ends
Of my loose locks 'twixt both your humid lips.
My hair is fallen now: knot it again!
SEBALD: I kiss you now, dear Ottima, now and now!   60
This way? Will you forgive me – be once more
My great queen?
OTTIMA: Bind it thrice about my brow;
Crown me your queen, your spirit's arbitress,
Magnificent in sin. Say that!

Robert Browning (1812–89), from *Pippa Passes*

Penelope

Penelope, initially suspicious of the man who has arrived in Ithaca claiming to be her long-lost husband Ulysses, craftily suggests that their bridal bed be brought into the hall. When Ulysses declares that the bed is formed from a growing oak, she realizes that he is, indeed, her husband.

While yet he speaks, her powers of life decay,
She sickens, trembles, falls, and faints away:
At length recovering, to his arms she flew,
And strained him close, as to his breast she grew;
The tears poured down amain, and, 'Oh,' she cries,   5
'Let not against thy spouse thine anger rise!
O versed in every turn of human art,
Forgive the weakness of a woman's heart!
The righteous powers that mortal lots dispose,
Decree us to sustain a length of woes,   10
And from the flower of life the bliss deny
To bloom together, fade away, and die.
O let me, let me not thine anger move,
That I forbore, thus, thus, to speak my love;

Thus in fond kisses, while the transport warms,   15
Pour out my soul, and die within thy arms!
I dreaded fraud! Men, faithless men, betray
Our easy faith, and make the sex their prey.
Against the fondness of my heart I strove,
'Twas caution, O my lord, not want of love!   20
Like me had Helen feared, with wanton charms
Ere the fair mischief set two worlds in arms,
Ere Greece rose dreadful in th' avenging day,
Thus had she feared, she had not gone astray.
But heaven, averse to Greece, in wrath decreed   25
That she should wander, and that Greece should bleed!
Blind to the ills that from injustice flow;
She coloured all our wretched lives with woe.
But why these sorrows, when my lord arrives?
I yield, I yield! My own Ulysses lives!   30
The secrets of the bridal bed are known
To thee, to me, to Actoris alone,
(My father's present in the spousal hour,
The sole attendant on our genial bower).
Since what no eye has seen thy tongue revealed,   35
Hard and distrustful as I am, I yield.'

Alexander Pope (1688–1744), translated from
Homer's *Odyssey*, Book XXIII

Portia

*Portia resents her exclusion from the troubles of her husband, the
noble Roman Brutus, who has become involved in the conspiracy
against Caesar.*

PORTIA: Is Brutus sick? and is it physical
         To walk unbraced and suck up the humours
         Of the dank morning? What? Is Brutus sick,
         And will he steal out of his wholesome bed,
         To dare the vile contagion of the night,   5
         And tempt the rheumy and unpurgèd air

To add unto his sickness? No, my Brutus;
You have some sick offence within your mind,
Which, by the right and virtue of my place,
I ought to know of: and, upon my knees,   10
I charm you, by my once-commended beauty,
By all your vows of love, and that great vow
Which did incorporate and make us one,
That you unfold to me, yourself, your half,
Why you are heavy, and what men tonight   15
Have had to resort to you: for here have been
Some six or seven, who did hide their faces
Even from darkness.
BRUTUS: Kneel not, gentle Portia.
PORTIA: I should not need, if you were gentle Brutus.
Within the bond of marriage, tell me, Brutus,   20
Is it excepted I should know no secrets
That appertain to you? Am I yourself
But, as it were, in sort or limitation,
To keep with you at meals, comfort your bed,
And talk to you sometimes? Dwell I but in the
    suburbs   25
Of your good pleasure? If it be no more,
Portia is Brutus' harlot, not his wife.

William Shakespeare (1564–1616), from
Julius Caesar, Act II

A 'Portuguese Lady'

*The Portuguese Lady speaks of the difficulty of articulating her
love, and of the need for love to triumph over everyday
circumstances.*

(1)

And wilt thou have me fashion into speech
The love I bear thee, finding words enough,
And hold the torch out, while the winds are rough,
Between our faces, to cast light on each? –
I drop it at thy feet. I cannot teach   5

My hand to hold my spirit so far off
From myself – me – that I should bring thee proof
In words, of love hid in me out of reach.
Nay, let the silence of my womanhood
Commend my woman-love to thy belief, –   10
Seeing that I stand unwon, however wooed,
And rend the garment of my life, in brief,
By a most dauntless, voiceless fortitude,
Lest one touch of this heart convey its grief.

                              (2)

If thou must love me, let it be for nought
Except for love's sake only. Do not say
'I love her for her smile – her look – her way
Of speaking gently, – for a trick of thought
That falls in well with mine, and certes brought   5
A sense of pleasant ease on such a day' –
For these things in themselves, belovèd, may
Be changed, or change for thee, – and love, so wrought,
May be unwrought so. Neither love me for
Thine own dear pity's wiping my cheeks dry, –   10
A creature might forget to weep, who bore
Thy comfort long, and lose thy love thereby!
But love me for love's sake, that evermore
Thou may'st love on, through love's eternity.

                        Elizabeth Barrett Browning (1806–61), from
                                        Sonnets from the Portuguese

Sappho

The poet Sappho writes to her lover, the maiden Philaenis.

Where is that holy fire, which verse is said
            To have? Is that enchanting force decayed?
Verse that draws nature's works from nature's law,
            Thee, her best work, to her work cannot draw.

Have my tears quenched my old poetic fire;   5
     Why quenched they not as well, that of desire?
Thoughts, my mind's creatures, often are with thee,
     But I, their maker, want their liberty.
Only thine image, in my heart, doth sit,
     But that is wax, and fires environ it.   10
My fires have driven, thine have drawn it hence;
     And I am robbed of picture, heart, and sense.
Dwells with me still mine irksome memory,
     Which both to keep and lose grieves equally.
That tells me how fair thou art: thou art so fair   15
     As gods, when gods to thee I do compare,
Are graced thereby; and to make blind men see,
     What things gods are, I say they are like to thee.
For, if we justly call each silly man
     A little world, what shall we call thee then?   20
Thou art not soft, and clear, and straight, and fair,
     As down, as stars, as cedars, and lilies are,
But thy right hand and cheek and eye only
     Are like thy other hand and cheek and eye.
Such was my Phao awhile, but shall be never,   25
     As thou, wast, art, and, oh, may'st thou be ever.
Here lovers swear in their idolatry,
     That I am such; but grief discolours me.
And yet I grieve the less, lest grief remove
     My beauty, and make me unworthy of thy love.   30
Plays some soft boy with thee, oh there wants yet
     A mutual feeling which should sweeten it.
His chin, a thorny hairy unevenness
     Doth threaten, and some daily change possess.
Thy body is a natural paradise,   35
     In whose self, unmanured, all pleasure lies,
Nor needs perfection; why shouldst thou then
     Admit the tillage of a harsh rough man?
Men leave behind them that which their sin shows,
     And are as thieves traced, which rob when it
          snows.   40
But of our dalliance no more signs there are,
     Than fishes leave in streams, or birds in air.
And between us all sweetness may be had;
     All, all that nature yields, or art can add.

My two lips, eyes, thighs, differ from thy two,   45
    But so, as thine from one another do;
And, oh, no more; the likeness being such,
    Why should they not alike in all parts touch?
Hand to strange hand, lip to lip none denies;
    Why should they breast to breast, or thighs to
        thighs?   50
Likeness begets such strange self-flattery,
    That touching myself, all seems done to thee.
Myself I embrace, and mine own hands I kiss,
    And amorously thank myself for this.
Me, in my glass, I call thee; but alas,   55
    When I would kiss, tears dim mine eyes, and glass.
O cure this loving madness, and restore
    Me to me; thee, my half, my all, my more;
So may thy cheeks' red outwear scarlet dye,
    And their white, whiteness of the galaxy,   60
So may thy mighty, amazing beauty move
    Envy in all women, and in all men, love,
And so be change, and sickness, far from thee,
    As thou by coming near, keep'st them from me.

John Donne (1572–1631), 'Sappho to Philaenis'

Sigismonda

*Sigismonda, a young widow, has contracted a secret marriage with
Guiscardo, a squire to her father, Tancred. Tancred has had
Guiscardo arrested, and has rebuked Sigismonda for her conduct.
She responds to his charges.*

'Tancred, I neither am disposed to make
Request for life, nor offered life to take;
Much less deny the deed; but least of all
Beneath pretended justice weakly fall.
My words to sacred truth shall be confined,   5
My deeds shall show the greatness of my mind.

That I have loved, I own; that still I love,
I call to witness all the powers above:
Yet more I own: to Guiscard's love I give
The small remaining time I have to live;   10
And if beyond this life desire can be,
Not Fate itself shall set my passion free.
        This first avowed; nor folly warped my mind,
Nor the frail texture of the female kind
Betrayed my virtue; for too well I knew   15
What honour was, and honour had his due:
Before the holy priest my vows were tied,
So came I not a strumpet, but a bride.
This for my fame, and for the public voice;
Yet more, his merits justified my choice: 20
Which had they not, the first election thine,
That bond dissolved, the next is freely mine:
Or grant I erred – which yet I must deny –
Had parents power ev'n second vows to tie,
Thy little care to mend my widowed nights   25
Has forced me to recourse of marriage rites,
To fill an empty side, and follow known delights.
What have I done in this deserving blame?
State-laws may alter; nature's are the same;
Those are usurped on helpless womankind,   30
Made without our consent, and wanting power to bind.
        Thou, Tancred, better shouldst have understood,
That, as thy father gave thee flesh and blood,
So gavest thou me: not from the quarry hewed,
But of a softer mould, with sense endued;   35
Ev'n softer than thy own, of suppler kind,
More exquisite of taste, and more than man refined.
Nor need'st thou by thy daughter to be told,
Though now thy sprightly blood with age be cold,
Thou hast been young; and canst remember still,   40
That when thou hadst the power, thou hadst the will;
And from the past experience of thy fires,
Canst tell with what a tide our strong desires
Come rushing on in youth, and what their rage requires.
        And grant thy youth was exercised in arms,   45
When love no leisure found for softer charms,
My tender age in luxury was trained,

With idle ease and pageants entertained;
My hours my own, my pleasures unrestrained.
So bred, no wonder if I took the bent   50
That seemed ev'n warranted by thy consent;
For when the father is too fondly kind,
Such seed he sows, such harvest shall he find.
　　　Blame then thyself, as reason's law requires,
(Since nature gave, and thou foment'st my fires),   55
If still those appetites continue strong,
Thou may'st consider I am yet but young.
Consider too, that having been a wife,
I must have tasted of a better life;
And am not to be blamed if I renew   60
By lawful means the joys which then I knew.
Where was the crime if pleasure I procured;
Young, and a woman, and to bliss inured?
That was my case, and this is my defence:
I pleased myself, I shunned incontinence,   65
And, urged by strong desires, indulged my sense.'

John Dryden (1631–1700), from
'Sigismonda and Guiscardo', translated from
Boccaccio's *Decameron*, Day IV

Sybil

*Sybil, a strict Quaker's spirited daughter, is advised by her mother
on marriage.*

　　　'Hear me,' she said; 'incline thy heart, my child,
And fix thy fancy on a man so mild:
Thy father, Sybil, never could be moved
By one who loved him, or by one he loved.
Union like ours is but a bargain made   5
By slave and tyrant: he will be obeyed;
Then calls the quiet, comfort – but thy youth
Is mild by nature, and as frank as truth.'
　　　'But will he love?' said Sybil; 'I am told
That these mild creatures are by nature cold.'   10

'Alas!' the matron answered, 'much I dread
That dangerous love by which the young are led!
That love is earthy; you the creature prize,
And trust your feelings and believe your eyes:
Can eyes and feelings inward worth descry?   15
No, my fair daughter, on our choice rely!
Your love, like that displayed upon the stage,
Indulged is folly, and opposed is rage;
More prudent love our sober couples show,
All that to mortal beings, mortals owe;   20
All flesh is grass – before you give a heart,
Remember, Sybil, that in death you part;
And should your husband die before your love,
What needless anguish must a widow prove!
No, my fair child! Let all such visions cease;   25
Yield but esteem, and only try for peace.'
        'I must be loved,' said Sybil; 'I must see
The man in terrors who aspires to me;
At my forbidding frown his heart must ache,
His tongue must falter, and his frame must shake: 30
And if I grant him at my feet to kneel,
What trembling, fearful pleasure must he feel!
Nay, such the raptures that my smiles inspire,
That reason's self must for a time retire.'
        'Alas, for good Josiah!' said the dame,   35
'These wicked thoughts would fill his soul with shame;
He kneel and tremble at a thing of dust?
He cannot, child.' The child replied, 'He must!'

George Crabbe (1754–1832), from 'The Frank Courtship'

Sylvia

The song of the fifteen-year-old Sylvia.

1

Sylvia the fair, in the bloom of fifteen,
Felt an innocent warmth as she lay on the green;
She had heard of a pleasure, and something she guessed
By the tousing and tumbling and touching her breast.
She saw the men eager, but was at a loss,   5
What they meant by their sighing and kissing so close;
      By their praying and whining,
      And clasping and twining,
      And panting and wishing,
      And sighing and kissing,   10
      And sighing and kissing so close.

2

'Ah', she cried, 'ah, for a languishing maid,
In a country of Christians to die without aid!
Not a Whig or a Tory, or Trimmer at least,
Or a Protestant parson or Catholic priest,   15
To instruct a young virgin that is at a loss,
What they meant by their sighing and kissing so close!
      By their praying and whining,
      And clasping and twining,
      And panting and wishing,   20
      And sighing and kissing,
      And sighing and kissing so close.'

3

Cupid in shape of a swain did appear,
He saw the sad wound and in pity drew near;
Then showed her his arrow and bid her not fear,   25
For the pain was no more than a maiden may bear.
When the balm was infused, she was not at a loss
What they meant by their sighing and kissing so close;
      By their praying and whining,
      And clasping and twining,   30
      And panting and wishing,

And sighing and kissing,
And sighing and kissing so close.

John Dryden (1631–1700), 'A New Song'

Venus

The love goddess Venus woos the chaste youth Adonis.

Thus she replies: 'Thy palfrey, as he should,
Welcomes the warm approach of sweet desire:
Affection is a coal that must be cooled;
Else, suffered, it will set the heart on fire:
    The sea hath bounds, but deep desire hath none;   5
    Therefore no marvel though thy horse be gone.

How like a jade he stood, tied to the tree,
Servilely mastered with a leathern rein!
But when he saw his love, his youth's fair fee,
He held such petty bondage in disdain;   10
    Throwing the base thong from his bending crest,
    Enfranchising his mouth, his back, his breast.

Who sees his true-love in her naked bed,
Teaching the sheets a whiter hue than white,
But, when his glutton eye so full hath fed,   15
His other agents aim at like delight?
    Who is so faint, that dare not be so bold
    To touch the fire, the weather being cold?

Let me excuse thy courser, gentle boy;
And learn of him, I heartily beseech thee,   20
To take advantage on presented joy;
Though I were dumb, yet his proceedings teach thee.
    O learn to love, the lesson is but plain,
    And once made perfect, never lost again.'

'I know not love,' quoth he, 'nor will not know it,   25
Unless it be a boar, and then I chase it;
'Tis much to borrow, and I will not owe it;

My love to love is love but to disgrace it;
      For I have heard it is a life in death,
      That laughs and weeps, and all but with a breath.   30

Who wears a garment shapeless and unfinished?
Who plucks the bud before one leaf put forth?
If springing things be any jot diminished,
They wither in their prime, prove nothing worth;
      The colt that's backed and burdened being young   35
      Loseth his pride, and never waxeth strong.

You hurt my hand with wringing; let us part,
And leave this idle theme, this bootless chat:
Remove your siege from my unyielding heart;
To love's alarms it will not ope the gate: 40
      Dismiss your vows, your feignèd tears, your flattery;
      For where a heart is hard they make no battery.'

'What, canst thou talk?' quoth she, 'hast thou a tongue?
Oh would thou hadst not, or I had no hearing;
Thy mermaid's voice hath done me double wrong;   45
I had my load before, now pressed with bearing:
      Melodious discord, heavenly tune, harsh-sounding,
      Ear's deep-sweet music, and heart's deep-sore
                                wounding.

Had I no eyes but ears, my ears would love
That inward beauty and invisible;   50
Or were I deaf, thy outward parts would move
Each part in me that were but sensible:
      Though neither eyes nor ears, to hear nor see,
      Yet should I be in love by touching thee.

Say, that the sense of feeling were bereft me,   55
And that I could not see, nor hear, nor touch,
And nothing but the very smell were left me,
Yet would my love to thee be still as much;
      For from the still'tory of thy face excelling
      Comes breath perfumed that breedeth love by smelling.

But oh, what banquet wert thou to the taste,
Being nurse and feeder of the other four;
Would they not wish the feast might ever last,
And bid Suspicion double-lock the door,

Lest Jealousy, that sour, unwelcome guest,   65
Should, by his stealing in, disturb the feast?'

William Shakespeare (1564–1616), from *Venus and Adonis*

Viola

Viola, disguised as the page-boy Cesario, tells Duke Orsino about women's hopeless love.

VIOLA: But if she cannot love you, sir?
DUKE ORSINO: I cannot be so answered.
VIOLA: Sooth, but you must.
  Say that some lady, as perhaps there is,
  Hath for your love as great a pang of heart
  As you have for Olivia: you cannot love her;   5
  You tell her so; must she not then be answered?
DUKE ORSINO: There is no woman's sides
  Can bide the beating of so strong a passion
  As love doth give my heart; no woman's heart
  So big, to hold so much; they lack retention.   10
  Alas, their love may be called appetite,
  No motion of the liver, but the palate,
  That suffer surfeit, cloyment and revolt;
  But mine is all as hungry as the sea,
  And can digest as much: make no compare   15
  Between that love a woman can bear me
  And that I owe Olivia.
VIOLA: Ay, but I know –
DUKE ORSINO: What dost thou know?
VIOLA: Too well what love women to men may owe:
  In faith, they are as true of heart as we.   20
  My father had a daughter loved a man,
  As it might be, perhaps, were I a woman,
  I should your lordship.
DUKE ORSINO: And what's her history?
VIOLA: A blank, my lord. She never told her love,
  But let concealment, like a worm i' the bud,   25

Feed on her damask cheek: she pined in thought,
And with a green and yellow melancholy
She sat like Patience on a monument,
Smiling at grief. Was not this love indeed?
We men may say more, swear more: but indeed   30
Our shows are more than will; for still we prove
Much in our vows, but little in our love.
DUKE ORSINO: But died thy sister of her love, my boy?
VIOLA: I am all the daughters of my father's house,
And all the brothers too: and yet I know not.   35

William Shakespeare (1564–1616), from
Twelfth Night, Act II

A Widow

The widow, reflecting on her own experience in marriage, advises Nancy to resist romantic notions, and marry her honest farmer-suitor.

'Force, my young friend, when forty years are fled,
Is what a woman seldom has to dread;
She needs no brazen locks nor guarding walls,
And seldom comes a lover, though she calls:
Yet, moved by fancy, one approved my face,   5
Though time and tears had wrought it much disgrace.
       The man I married was sedate and meek,
And spoke of love as men in earnest speak;
Poor as I was, he ceaseless sought, for years,
A heart in sorrow and a face in tears: 10
That heart I gave not; and 'twas long before
I gave attention, and then nothing more;
But in my breast some grateful feeling rose,
For one whose love so sad a subject chose;
Till long delaying, fearing to repent,   15
But grateful still, I gave a cold assent.
       Thus we were wed; no fault had I to find,
And he but one; my heart could not be kind:
Alas! of every early hope bereft,

There was no fondness in my bosom left;   20
So had I told him, but had told in vain,
He lived but to indulge me and complain:
His was this cottage, he inclosed this ground,
And planted all these blooming shrubs around;
He to my room these curious trifles brought,   25
And with assiduous love my pleasure sought;
He lived to please me, and I ofttimes strove,
Smiling, to thank his unrequited love:
"Teach me," he cried, "that pensive mind to ease,
For all my pleasure is the hope to please."   30
Serene, though heavy, were the days we spent,
Yet kind each word, and generous each intent;
But his dejection lessened every day,
And to a placid kindness died away:
In tranquil ease we passed our latter years,   35
By griefs untroubled, unassailed by fears.
Let not romantic views your bosom sway,
Yield to your duties, and their call obey:
Fly not a youth, frank, honest, and sincere;
Observe his merits, and his passion hear!   40
'Tis true, no hero, but a farmer sues –
Slow in his speech, but worthy in his views;
With him you cannot that affliction prove,
That rends the bosom of the poor in love:
Health, comfort, competence, and cheerful days,   45
Your friends' approval, and your father's praise,
Will crown the deed, and you escape *their* fate
Who plan so wildly, and are wise too late.'

George Crabbe (1754–1832), from 'The Widow's Tale'

The Wife of Bath

(1)

The Wife of Bath speaks of virginity and chastity.

Virginity is great perfectïon,
And continence eek with devotïon.
But Christ, that of perfectïon is well,
Bade not every wight he should go sell
All that he had, and give it to the poor,   5
And in such wise follow him and his fore.
He spake to them that would live perfectly;
And, lordings, by your leave, that am not I.
I will bestow the flower of all my age
In th' actës and in fruit of marrïage.   10
        Tell me also, to what conclusïon
Were members made of generatïon,
And of so perfect wise a wright ywrought?
Trusteth right well, they were not made for nought.
Gloss whoso will, and say both up and down,   15
That they were makëd for purgatïon
Of urine, and our bothë thingës small
Were eek to know a female from a male,
And for no other causë: say ye no?
Th' experience wot well it is not so;   20
So that the clerkës be not with me wroth,
I say this, that they makëd been for both,
This is to say, for office, and for ease
Of engendrure, there we not God displease.
Why should men ellës in hir bookës set,   25
That man shall yieldë to his wife her debt?
Now wherewith should he make his payëment,
If he ne used his sely instrument?
Then were they made upon a creäture,
To purge uríne, and eek for éngendrure.   30
        But I say not that every wight is hold,
That hath such harness as I to you told,
To go and usë them in éngendrure;
Then should men take of chastity no cure.

Christ was a maid, and shapen as a man,   35
And many a saint, since that the world began;
Yet lived they ever in perfect chastity.
I nil envyë no virginity:
Let them be bred of purëd wheatë-seed,
And let us wivës hoten barley-bread;   40
And yet with barley-bread, Mark tellë can,
Our lord Jesú refreshëd many a man.
In such estate as God hath clepëd us
I will persever; I am not precious.
In wifehood I will use mine instrument   45
As freely as my Maker hath it sent.
If I be dangerous, God give me sorrow!
My husband shall it have both eve and morrow,
When that him list come forth and pay his debt.
An husband I will have, I will nat let,   50
Which shall be both my debtor and my thrall,
And have his tribulatïon withall
Upon his flesh, while that I am his wife.
I have the power during all my life
Upon his proper body, and not he.   55
Right thus th' Apostle told it unto me,
And bade our husbands for to love us well.
All this senténce me liketh everydeel'.

(2)

The Wife of Bath speaks of aged husbands.

Now, sires, then will I tell you forth my tale. –
As ever might I drinken wine or ale,
I shal say sooth, those husbands that I had,
As three of them were good and two were bad.
The three were goodë men, and rich, and old;   5
Unnethë mightë they the statute hold
In which that they were bounden unto me.
Ye woot well what I mean of this, pardee!
As help me God, I laughë when I think
How piteously a-night I made them swink;   10
And by my faith, I told of it no store.
They had me giv'n their gold and their treasúre;

Me needed not do longer diligence
To win their love, or do them reverence.
They lovëd me so well, by God above,   15
That I ne told no dainty of their love!
A wise woman will set her ever in one
To get her love, yea, theras she hath none.
But since I had them wholly in my hand,
And since they had me given all their land,   20
What should I takë keep them for to please,
But it were for my profit and my ease?
I set them so a-workë, by my fay,
That many a night they sungen 'wailaway!'
The bacon was not fet for them, I trow,   25
That some men have in Essex at Dunmow.
I governed them so well, after my law,
That each of them full blissful was and faw
To bring me gayë thingës from the fair.
They were full glad when I spake to them fair;   30
For, God it wot, I chid them spitously.

(3)

The Wife of Bath's fifth husband.

Now of my fifthë husband will I tell.
God let his soulë never come in hell!
And yet was he to me the mostë shrew;
That feel I on my ribbës all by rew,
And ever shall, unto mine ending day.   5
But in our bed he was so fresh and gay,
And therewithal so well could he me glose,
When that he wouldë have my *belle chose*,
That though he had me beat on every bone,
He couldë win again my love anon.   10
I trow I loved him bestë, for that he
Was of his lovë dangerous to me.
We women have, if that I shall not lie,
In this matter a quaintë fantasy;
Waitë what thing we may not lightly have,   15
Thereafter will we cry all day and crave.
Forbid us thing, and that desiren we;
Press on us fast, and thennë will we flee.

With danger outë we all our chaffare;
Great press at market maketh dearë ware,   20
And too great cheap is held at little price;
This knoweth every woman that is wise.

(4)

The Wife of Bath's life with Jankin.

To churchë was mine husband born amorrow
With neighëbours that for him maden sorrow,
And Jankin ourë clerk was one of tho.
As help me God, when that I saw him go
After the bier, methought he had a pair   5
Of leggës and of feet so clean and fair,
That all my heart I gave unto his hold.
He was, I trow, a twenty winter old,
And I was forty, if I shall say sooth;
But yet I had alway a coltë's tooth.   10
Gat-toothed I was, and that became me well;
I had the print of Saintë Venus' seal.
As help me God, I was a lusty one,
And fair and rich and young, and well begun;
And truly, as mine husbands toldë me,   15
I had the bestë *quoniam* mightë be.
For certes, I am all Venerian
In feeling, and mine heart is Martïan.
Venus me gave my lust, my licorousness,
And Mars gave me my sturdy hardiness.   20
Mine áscendent was Taur, and Mars therein.
Alas! alas! that ever love was sin!
I followed aye mine inclinatïon
By virtue of my constellatïon;
That madë me I couldë not withdraw   25
My chamber of Venus from a good fellów.
Yet have I Mars's mark upon my face,
And also in another privy place.
For, God so wise be my salvatïon,
I ne loved never by no discretïon,   30
But ever followëd my appetite,
All were he short or long, or black or white;

I took no keep, so that he likëd me,
How poor he was, ne eek of what degree.

Geoffrey Chaucer (*c.* 1343–1400), from
'The Wife of Bath's Prologue'

Xantippe

Xantippe remembers her first meeting with her future husband, the philosopher Socrates.

Once, walking 'thwart the crowded market-place,
With other maidens, bearing in the twigs
White doves for Aphrodite's sacrifice,
I saw him, all ungainly and uncouth,
Yet many gathered round to hear his words,   5
Tall youths and stranger-maidens – Socrates –
I saw his face and marked it, half in awe,
Half with a quick repulsion at the shape . . .
The richest gem lies hidden furthest down,
And is the dearer for the weary search;   10
We grasp the shining shells which strew the shore,
Yet swift we fling them from us; but the gem
We keep for aye and cherish. So a soul,
Found after weary searching in the flesh
Which half repelled our senses, is more dear,   15
For that same seeking, than the sunny mind
Which lavish Nature marks with thousand hints
Upon a brow of beauty. We are prone
To overweigh such subtle hints, then deem,
In after disappointment, we are fooled   20
And when, at length, my father told me all,
That I should wed me with great Socrates,
I, foolish, wept to see at once cast down
The maiden image of a future love,
Where perfect body matched the perfect soul.   25
But slowly, softly did I cease to weep;
Slowly I 'gan to mark the magic flash
Leap to the eyes, to watch the sudden smile
Break round his mouth, and linger in the eyes;
To listen for the voice's lightest tone –   30

Great voice, whose cunning modulations seemed
Like to the notes of some sweet instrument.
So did I reach and strain, until at last
I caught the soul athwart the grosser flesh.
Again of thee, sweet Hope, my spirit dreamed!   35
I, guided by his wisdom and his love,
Led by his words, and counselled by his care,
Should lift the shrouding veil from things which be,
And at the flowing fountain of his soul
Refresh my thirsting spirit . . . .
               And indeed   40
In those long days which followed that strange day
When rites and song, and sacrifice and flowers,
Proclaimed that we were wedded, did I learn,
In sooth, a-many lessons; bitter ones
Which sorrow taught me, and not love inspired,   45
Which deeper knowledge of my kind impressed
With dark insistence on reluctant brain; –
But that great wisdom, deeper, which dispels
Narrowed conclusions of a half-grown mind,
And sees athwart the littleness of life   50
Nature's divineness and her harmony,
Was never poor Xantippe's . . . .
             I would pause
And would recall no more, no more of life,
Than just the incomplete, imperfect dream
Of early summers, with their light and shade,   55
Their blossom-hopes, whose fruit was never ripe;
But something strong within me, some sad chord
Which loudly echoes to the later life,
Me to unfold the after-misery
Urges, with plaintive wailing in my heart.   60
Yet, maidens, mark; I would not that ye thought
I blame my lord departed, for he meant
No evil, so I take it, to his wife.
'Twas only that the high philosopher,
Pregnant with noble theories and great thoughts,   65
Deigned not to stoop to touch so slight a thing
As the fine fabric of a woman's brain –
So subtle as a passionate woman's soul.

    Amy Levy (1861–89), from 'Xantippe: A Fragment'

Notes

Andromache **2 son:** Astyanax. **11 tenor:** course. **15 Achilles:** chief warrior among the Greeks. **16 Thebè:** Thebes, kingdom of Andromache's father, Aëtion, who, along with Andromache's brothers, was slain by Achilles. **20 decent:** in a fitting manner. **23 Jove's sylvan daughters:** trees appropriate to surround a tomb. **28 hapless:** unlucky. **30 Hippoplacia:** Mount Hippoplacus overlooked Thebes. **34 Diana:** goddess of the chase. **44 Agamemnon:** leader of the Greek forces at Troy. **45 Tydides:** Diomedes. **Ajax:** with Diomedes, one of the leading Greek warriors. **46 the vengeful Spartan:** Menelaus, the seizure of whose wife, Helen, by Paris caused the Trojan War. **48 Or:** either. **55 Attaint:** defame. **65 presage:** presentiment. **67 hoary:** white. **71 Argive:** Agamemnon was King of Argos. **74 Hyperia:** a spring in Argos. **82 clay:** earth (forming a tomb).

Arabella **(1) 19 wretch:** cast-off mistress. **20 spurious:** bastard. **(2) 8 stay:** wait. **35 careless of:** not caring about. **45 That daring sex:** men. **slight:** not regard seriously. **53 upbraid:** rebuke. **57 vicious:** sinful, corrupt.

Ariadne **6 flame:** love. **17 clew:** thread (by means of which Ariadne helped Theseus escape from the Labyrinth). **21–4:** the references are to the celebrated mythological torments inflicted on Prometheus (on whose liver an eagle fed daily), Sisyphus (condemned to roll a stone repeatedly to the top of a hill) and Ixion (bound to a constantly revolving fiery wheel). **28 woof:** woven fabric. **36 Took:** bewitched. **42 several:** various. **44 shell:** Venus, said to have been born from the foam, was sometimes depicted floating on the waves on a scallop shell. **46 Venture:** risk (the reference is to the net in which Venus and Mars were caught *in flagrante*, and exposed to the ridicule of the gods).

Asia **5 conducting:** steering. **14 pinions:** wings. **20 Elysian:** blessed (from Elysium, Homer's 'Islands of the Blessed'). **22 pinnace:** small boat. **38 like thee:** i.e. the bright lamps are like Prometheus.

Aurora Leigh **(1) 14 Hagar:** concubine of Abraham, never raised to the proper status of wife (Genesis 16). **17 chief apostle:** St Paul, said to have advocated women's chaste service to their husbands in missionary work.   **30 Graces:** minor goddesses who personify grace and beauty and accompany the Muses, goddesses of the arts.   **50 oakum:** rope used to caulk ships, 'picked' (unravelled) by criminals and paupers.   **84 Fouriers:** the eccentric socialist Charles Fourier (1772–1837) had advocated the organization of society into 'phalansteries', communal associations with complex patterns of hierarchy. **(2) 11 inflatus:** breathing out, inspiration.   **23 in Leone:** in the sign of the zodiac entered by the sun in late July.   **26 captious:** carping.

Belinda   1 th' etherial plain: the sky.

Britomart   1 fortunèd: chanced.   **2 repair:** go.   **6 in vain:** with no particular purpose.   **7 Though:** then. **avizing of:** considering.   **9 that:** that which.   **10 falleth:** happens.   **13 buxom:** obedient.   **18 wist:** knew.   **19 Eftsoons:** immediately.   **20 wise:** manner.   **21 ventayle:** front of helmet.   **22 agrize:** terrify.   **24 Phoebus:** Apollo, the sun god.   **26 Portly:** stately, handsome.   **27 gest:** demeanour.   **31 yfretted:** adorned with fretwork.   **35 ermelin:** ermine.   **36 pouldred:** spotted.   **38 fastened:** fixed her thoughts.   **38 ne:** nor did. **39 unguilty:** unsuspecting.   **40 ween:** think.   **42 unwist:** unknown.   **43 the false archer:** Cupid.   **45 weetless:** unconscious. **stound:** grief.   **47 Ruffèd:** ruffled. **avail:** droop.   **48 portance:** carriage. **gest:** demeanour.   **49 erst:** formerly. **51 wox:** grew. **52 silly:** innocent. **she did ail:** ailed her.   **53 perdy:** truly.   **57 reft:** taken.   **63 closely:** secretly.   **65 still:** drop. **sprite:** spirit.   **70 affright:** frightened. **71 Tho gan she:** then she began.

Circe   10 Apollo: god of music.   **11 peered:** equalled.   **22 these:** the ordinary men whom she has transformed into beasts.   **23 mop:** drink greedily. **mow:** grimace.   **24 byres:** cowsheds.   **32 basilisks:** mythical reptiles whose breath and stare was fatal.

Clarissa   6 side-box: boxes in the theatre from which men could view the ladies in the front-boxes which faced the stage. **15 patch:** wear a cosmetic patch on the face. **become:** be becoming in.   **16 paint:** wear make-up.   **24 flights:** fits of unreasonable caprice or temper.

Cleopatra   (1) 1 Charmian: Cleopatra's maid.   **5 bravely:** excellently. **wot'st:** knowest.   **6 demi-Atlas:** half-Atlas (because he supports half the world).   **7 burgonet:** helmet (i.e. protector).   **11 Phoebus':** the sun god's.   **12 fronted:** browed. **Caesar:** Julius Caesar, formerly Cleopatra's lover.   **14 Pompey:** Gnaeus Pompey, son of Pompey the

Great. **16 aspect:** gaze. **(2) 8 Crested:** was raised above (as in heraldry). **8–9 propertied/As:** possessed with the harmony of. **15–16 in ... crownets:** kings and princes were his servants. **17 plates:** silver coins. **22 wants:** lacks. **23 vie ... fancy:** compete with imagination in creating wonderful objects. **24 piece 'gainst:** masterpiece in competition with. **25 shadows:** mere imaginings. **28 O'ertake:** achieve. **but:** unless. **29 rebound:** reflection. **(3) 4 Yare:** quickly. **8 their:** the gods'. **9 title:** right. **13 Iras:** another of Cleopatra's servants. **14 aspic:** asp. **22 curlèd:** curly-haired. **23 make demand of:** ask for news of. **25 intrinsicate:** intricate. **29 Unpolicied:** outwitted. **37 Phoebus:** the sun god.

Criseyde **(1) 2 eek:** also. **gentilesse:** noble behaviour. **3 All:** although. **nought to done:** not to be done. **6 In honesty:** honourably. **7 estate:** standing. **heal:** health. **8 wot:** know. **11 Paraunter:** perhaps. **despite:** anger, resentment. **14 there I may:** where I could. **17 nought forbet:** does not forbid. **23 thewës:** habits. **nice:** foolish. **24 avantour:** boaster. **26 als:** also. **nil:** will not. **27 avaunt:** boast. **28 clause:** article. **29 set a case:** assume a situation. **ywis:** I know, indeed. **30 deemë:** think. **32 let:** hinder. **33 all day:** constantly. **34 beside their leave:** without their permission. **35 them list:** it pleases them. **let them leave:** leave them alone. **37 thriftiest:** best-conducted woman. **38 so:** if. **40 Hector:** noblest of the Trojan warriors. **41 cure:** care. **42 my áventure:** my lot, my fortune. **45 All:** although. **wist of:** know about. **46 one the fairestë:** singly the most fair. **out of dread:** doubtless. **49 though:** if. **52 lease:** pastures. **53 debate:** strife. **56 masterful:** domineering. **novelry:** novelty. **57 fine:** end. **58 in case if that me lest:** if it pleases me. **59 religïous:** a nun. **(2) 4 Phoebus:** the sun. **5 fere:** mate. **8 grave:** engraved. **10 wisely:** surely. **11 the pain:** torture. **17 wistë soothly:** knew truly. **18 eech:** increase. **20 Beth:** be. **ruth:** pity. **22 forthy:** therefore. **sickerness:** security. **23 mo:** others. **27 As wisely:** as surely as. **(3) 3 falsëd:** betrayed. **4 clean ago:** completely lost. **6 one the gentilest:** singly the finest man. **10 shend:** destroy. **14 fall:** happen to. **16 weylaway:** alas. **17 All:** although. **20 rue:** regret. **21 algate:** at any rate. **23 departen:** part. **27 lady:** lady's. **29 certes:** certainly. **38 ween:** suppose. **40 termë:** period of time. **dread:** doubt. **43 Ne me ne list:** nor does it please me to. **sely:** poor. **49 Ywis:** indeed. **ruth:** pity.

Dalilah **4–5 mutable/Of fancy:** changeable in your inclinations. **6 her**

at Timna: Samson's first wife, who also betrayed him, and was given away by Samson's father-in-law. **23 fond:** foolish.

Desdemona 8 Delighted them: took delight in. **9 yet:** still. **12 forswear me:** give me up. **16 addition:** designation.

Dido (1) 9 Tyrrhene sea: sea lying between Italy and Corsica, Sardinia and Sicily. **13 Ascanius:** Aeneas' son. **22 vowed:** determined. **26 empery:** empire. **(2) 4 Hyrcanian:** from Hyrcania, near the Caspian Sea. **13 equal:** fair. **21 A god's command:** Mercury has ordered Aeneas to leave Carthage and pursue his Italian quest. **23 Lycian lots:** oracles of Apollo.

Dolly (text based on *Poems Descriptive of Rural Life and Scenery* (1820)) **4 brushed off:** moved off briskly. **6 wake:** parish fair. **7 fairing:** present bought at a fair. **14 mun:** must. **23 whetting:** sharpening their scythes. **49 Merry-Andrew:** clown, popular entertainer. **51 fleering:** with mocking laughter. **86 ding'd:** hit (metaphorically).

The Duchess of Malfi 3 doubles: acts deceitfully. **24 quietus est:** discharge (from debt).

Elaine 16 bode: stayed. **33 still:** always. **39 quit:** recompense.

Eloisa 6 lambent: softly radiant. **8 mended:** improved. **19 wait:** attend. **53 matin:** morning. **56 bead:** (of Eloisa's rosary). **57 censer:** vessel from which incense is dispensed. **68 dispute:** contend for.

Emilia 3 foreign: of other women. **6 scant:** reduce. **having:** allowance. **7 galls:** tempers. **9 sense:** senses.

Erminia 1 doubtful: uncertain in outcome. **3 These:** the Christians. **4 Those:** the Saracens. **9 hapless:** unlucky. **18 list:** wished. **22 wist:** knew. **30 vesture:** clothing. **35 plained:** lamented. **38 forbear:** give up. **41 sely:** innocent. **42 mote:** speck of dust. **Phoebus':** the sun's. **46 assays:** attacks. **54 curious:** inquisitive. **63 disputed of:** reflected on. **69 suspect:** suspicion. **74 eftsoons:** soon. **97 for:** because. **98 virtue:** healing power.

Eve (1) 22 shadow: image. **stays:** waits for. **30 platan:** plane tree. **(2) 4 charm:** blended chorus. **6 orient:** rising. **9 grateful:** pleasing. **(3) 3 unweeting:** unintentionally. **8 stay:** support. **13 doom:** fate, judgement.

Francesca da Rimini 9 thy teacher: Virgil, who is leading Dante on his journey through Hell. **14 Lancelot:** the reference is to the kiss which, according to the romance of *Lancelot*, commenced the knight's guilty liaison with Queen Guinevere. **19 her:** Guinevere. **26 thralls:** bonds.

Griselda **1 dowér:** dowry. **6 visage:** facial expression. **8 sooth:** truth. **algate:** in any case. **10 not old as:** not the same when it is old as. **11 certes:** truly. **14 in whole intent:** whole-heartedly. **15 woot:** know. **16 weed:** clothing. **18 dread:** doubt. **21 eek:** also. **26 fain:** gladly. **30 thilkë:** the same. **36 guerdon:** recompense. **38 to my meed:** as my reward. **40 wry:** cover. **45 unnethës:** with difficulty. **46 ruth:** pity.

Guinevere **2 oriel-embowering:** woven round the oriel window-recess to form a bower. **6 gems:** diamonds won by Lancelot in a joust, and presented to Guinevere. **14 one:** King Arthur. **20 your new fancy:** Elaine. **31 haggard:** gaunt, scraggy. **45 maid of Astolat:** Elaine, who has died of grief, and is being conducted down the river in a barge.

Haidée **27 our first parents:** Adam and Eve. **30 the Stygian river:** principal river of the classical Underworld. **51 the Host:** bread consecrated in the Eucharist, and elevated during the service. **68 rude:** rough.

Helen of Troy **13 Atrides:** Menelaus, Helen's former husband, from whom she was abducted by Paris. **24 Phrygian:** Trojan. **27 Paphian queen:** Venus (born on Paphos).

Helena (1) **2 she:** Hermia. **7 quantity:** shape, proportion. **9 the mind:** mental fantasy. **11 taste:** trace. **12 figure:** symbolize. **15 game:** sport, play. **17 eyne:** eyes. **(2) 1 speak you fair:** speak kindly to you. **16 impeach:** call in question. **20 desert:** deserted. **22 privilege:** protection. **for that:** because. **26 in my respect:** as far as I am concerned. **29 brakes:** thickets. **33 Apollo flies:** (reversing the classical myth, in which the chaste Daphne fled the advances of the god Apollo, and was transformed into a laurel). **35 bootless:** useless. **37 stay:** await. **42 set a scandal on:** (by forcing her to behave in an 'unwomanly' manner).

Hero (1) **2 turtles':** turtle doves'. **28 hardly:** with difficulty. **(2) 2 jar:** argue. **16 whist:** silent. **19 Morpheus:** god of sleep. **23 beldame:** old woman. **32 assays:** tries.

Donna Julia **(1) 31 Armida:** a sorceress in Tasso's *Jerusalem Delivered*. **62 Tarquin:** son of the King of Rome; responsible for the rape of the virtuous Lucretia. **(2) 54 'Elle vous suit partout':** 'She follows you everywhere'. **55 cornelian:** a semi-transparent quartz, used for seals.

Julia, Daughter of Augustus **11 list:** wishes. **22 officious:** busy.

Juliet **9:** Juliet has declared her love for Romeo, without realizing that he is listening. **10 form:** propriety. **16 pronounce:** declare. **19 So:** as long as. **20 fond:** infatuated. **21 light:** frivolous, loose. **23 strange:** aloof. **27 not:** do not. **28 discoverèd:** revealed. **39 contract:** exchange of promises. **40 unadvised:** ill-considered.

Katharina **5 Confounds:** ruins. **fame:** reputation. **7 moved:** angry. **22 froward:** perversely disobedient. **peevish:** obstinate and wilful. **34 unable:** weak. **36 haply:** perhaps. **41:** Then lower your pride, for it is useless. **44 do him ease:** give him pleasure.

A Lady (1) **4 eke:** also. **8 freight:** laden. **14 avail:** disembarkation. **22 in arms across:** embracing. **31 fancies:** imaginings. **37 fro:** from. **38 plain:** complaint.

A Lady (3) **9 free:** irresponsible. **17 faith:** trust in love. **26 of yore:** in the past.

Lydia **4 towers:** tall headdresses. **10 the 'Change:** the Exchange, a fashionable place for business and social meetings. **12 antic:** eccentric. **China's azure:** the reference is to Chinese blue porcelain. **16 raffling:** gaming. **20 toy:** gift. **25 Poll:** Lydia's pet parrot. **27 Pug:** Lydia's lap-dog. **44 miss:** mistress. **for breed:** to beget children. **50 humours:** bad temper.

Madeline **St Agnes' Eve:** it was believed that if a girl went to bed supperless on St Agnes' Eve, she would receive a vision of her lover. **8 affrayed:** frightened. **35 alarum:** warning sign. **37 flaw-blown:** driven by the wind. **48 vermeil:** scarlet. **56 haggard:** wild, fierce. **58 bloated wassaillers:** revellers in Madeline's father's castle. **61 Rhenish:** Rhine wine.

Margaret **(1) 4 wist not:** did not know. **(2) 26 truant:** wandering. **32 but:** except.

Mariana **18 trance:** throw into a trance. **20 athwart:** across. **flats:** level country. **40 marish:** marsh.

Medea **39 My magic:** Medea was a renowned sorceress.

Medora Trevilian **6 the Po:** river in north Italy. **15 Orlando:** hero of Ariosto's romantic epic, *Orlando Furioso*. **17 top-boot:** high riding-boot, with a light-coloured top. **18 cob:** short-legged horse, ridden by fat people. **31 Werther:** the sensitive, melancholy artist-hero of a cele-brated novel by Goethe.

Monna Innominata Two poems from a sequence of sonnets imagining the sentiments of an unnamed Italian lady. **(2) 4 idle:** frivolous.

Myrrha 56 th' infernal bands: the Furies.

Ottima 5 simplicity: openness, honesty. **16 campanula:** bell-flower. **26 sere:** dry. **31 o'erblowed:** blown down. **32 suffered:** allowed to. **41 at a venture:** by chance.

Penelope 4 strained: embraced. **5 amain:** copiously. **32 Actoris:** their servant. **34 genial:** bridal.

Portia 1 physical: beneficial to your health. **2 unbraced:** with open tunic. **humours:** dampness. **6 tempt:** risk. **rheumy and unpurgèd:** dank and impure. **8 offence:** disturbance. **9 virtue:** prerogative. **place:** position as your wife. **11 charm:** conjure. **15 heavy:** depressed. **21 excepted:** stipulated as a condition in our marriage-contract. **23 in ... limitation:** with restrictions. **25 suburbs:** (where brothels were situated).

A 'Portuguese Lady' Two of a sequence of sonnets in which the 'Portuguese Lady' is a thinly disguised *persona* for Elizabeth Brown-ing. **(2) 5 certes:** indeed.

Sappho 3: (as Orpheus' verse caused animate and inanimate things to abandon their 'natural' behaviour). **4 work:** love. **8 want:** lack. **10 environ:** surround. **16 As:** that. **19 silly:** ordinary. **25 Phao:** Sappho's legendary (male) lover. **31 wants:** is lacking. **37 perfec-tion:** (such as would, supposedly, be supplied by a male lover). **59 outwear:** (because immortalized in Sappho's verse?).

Sigismonda 21 election: choice. **63 inured:** accustomed. **65 incontinence:** unchastity.

Sybil 18 rage: madness. **24 prove:** display.

Sylvia 4 tousing: pulling, tugging. **14 Trimmer:** political opportunist who changes sides according to which political party is in the ascendant.

Venus 1 palfrey: horse (Adonis' horse has been pursuing Venus' mare). **3 Affection:** passion. **4 suffered:** allowed to continue. **7 jade:** nag, without spirit. **9 fee:** reward. **16 agents:** faculties. **19 courser:** horse. **21 on:** of. **22 Though:** even if. **24 made perfect:** mastered by heart. **28 but:** only. **disgrace:** discredit.

33 springing: immature. **35 backed:** ridden. **38 idle:** useless. **bootless:** pointless. **40 alarms:** attacks. **42 battery:** breach. **46 pressed:** oppressed. **52 sensible:** sensitive. **59 still'tory:** still (used for making perfume). **excelling:** extremely beautiful.

Viola   1 she: Olivia, with whom Orsino is in love.   **2 be so answered:** have my courtship thus received. **Sooth:** truly.   **8 bide:** endure. **10 retention:** constancy.   **13 cloyment:** surfeit. **revolt:** revulsion. **17 owe:** bear.   **26 damask:** pink and white, like a damask rose. **31 shows:** displays of love. **will:** our desire. **still:** always.

A Widow   4 though: even if.   **45 competence:** financial security.

The Wife of Bath   (1) 2 eek: also.   **3 well:** the source.   **4 wight:** person.   **6 fore:** footsteps.   **13 of:** by. **wright:** maker. **yrought:** made.   **15 Gloss:** interpret.   **20 wot:** knows.   **21 So that:** provided that. **clerkës:** scholars.   **23 office:** service (of excretion).   **24 éngendrure:** begetting.   **26 yieldë:** pay.   **28 sely:** innocent.   **31 hold:** bound.   **34 cure:** heed.   **35 maid:** virgin.   **39 purëd:** refined. **wheatëm seed:** wheat-grain flour.   **40 hoten:** be called.   **43 clepëd:** called.   **44 precious:** fastidious.   **46 freely:** generously.   **47 dangerous:** standoffish.   **49 him list:** he wants to.   **50 nat let:** not refrain.   **51 thrall:** slave.   **55 proper:** own.   **58 senténce:** purport. **me liketh everydeel:** pleases me entirely.   **(2) 3 sooth:** truth. **6 Unnethë:** scarcely.   **10 swink:** work (sexually). **11 told ... store:** reckoned it at not much.   **16 told no dainty of:** set no store by. **17 ever in one:** constantly.   **25 trow:** believe.   **26 Dunmow:** the 'Dunmow flitch' of bacon was awarded to married couples who hadn't quarrelled for a year.   **28 faw:** glad.   **31 it wot:** knows. **spitously:** cruelly.   **(3) 3 shrew:** unkind.   **4 by rew:** in a row.   **7 glose:** wheedle.   **11 trow:** know.   **12 dangerous:** hard to get.   **15 Waitë what:** look at whatever. **lightly:** easily.   **19 outë:** spread out. **chaffare:** merchandise.   **20 dearë ware:** expensive goods.   **21 too great cheap:** too good a bargain.   **(4) 1 mine husband:** her fourth husband. **amorrow:** in the morning.   **3 tho:** those.   **6 clean:** neat.   **7 hold:** possession.   **10 coltë's tooth:** youthful appetite.   **11 Gat-toothed:** with a gap between my front teeth (supposedly a sign of lechery). **12 print:** birthmark.   **14 begun:** situated.   **18 Martïan:** devoted to Mars.   **19 licorousness:** lecherousness.   **21 áscendent:** horoscope. **Taur:** Taurus.   **24 constellation:** horoscope.   **32 All were he:** whether he was.   **33 keep:** heed. **so that:** as long as.   **34: eek:** also. **degree:** standing, class.

Xantippe   34 athwart: across.

Index of Poets